WITCHCRAFT
IN THE SOUTHWEST

*Spanish and Indian Supernaturalism
on the Rio Grande*

BY MARC SIMMONS

University of Nebraska Press
Lincoln and London

First Bison Book printing: 1980
Most recent printing indicated by first digit below:

8   9   10

Library of Congress Cataloging in Publication Data

Simmons, Marc.
  Witchcraft in the Southwest.

  Reprint of the ed. published by Northland Press, Flagstaff.
  Bibliography: p. 181
  1. Witchcraft—Southwest, New. 2. Indians of North America—Southwest,
New—Magic. I. Title.
[BF1577.S68S56 1980]   133.4′09789   79–18928
ISBN 0–8032–9116–7

Published by arrangement with the author
Manufactured in the United States of America

For four charming ladies
(who are anything but witches)
Eddie, Judy, Lili,
and Marianne

contents

ILLUSTRATIONS

PREFACE

IN THE REALM OF SERIOUS HISTORY, the story of witchcraft
is usually disposed of quickly with passing reference to the
European crazes of the fifteenth through the eighteenth centuries, or to the much condemned and frequently examined
madness that infected Salem, Massachusetts, in the latter
1600s. Because scholars seldom manifest an affinity for the
occult, they have tended to neglect the inescapable fact that
the mass of men are firmly wedded to belief in supernatural
phenomena and that the relentless rush of history is often
directed by the unbridled force of superstitious conviction.
Regardless of the direction of scholarly approach, however, it
cannot be disputed that witchery remains a subject of endless
fascination for a large segment of our population. In fact,
recent resurgence of interest in the occult has raised it almost
to the level of a popular fad. Perhaps the intent of any
thoughtful study should be the simple one of describing the
nature of witchcraft belief and the social consequences that
follow as men surrender their souls and powers of reason to
the baleful influence of the black arts. In such a study little
purpose is served by trying to show that the existence of
witchcraft cannot be scientifically established.

The present work surveys, from a historical rather than
from a strictly analytical point of view, the nature of witchcraft belief in that corner of the United States generally
known as the far Southwest. The Rio Grande, extending more
than a thousand miles from its mouth on the Texas Gulf

coast to its gushing headwaters in the southern Rockies of Colorado, defines the heartland of this region, and in both a literal and figurative sense nourishes the diverse peoples residing within its valley or along its tributary arms. Here Hispanic and Indian cultures intermingle and cope with the aggressive intrusion of "Anglos," who boldly assert the superiority of their own system and disparage the usefulness of time-honored folkways.

Aside from Clyde Kluckhohn's authoritative and technically detailed treatment of Navajo witchcraft, no book has delved below the surface of supernaturalism in the Southwest, nor has any volume attempted to encompass the broad outlines of the subject in a meaningful overview. In the pages that follow, the author has tried to accomplish these ends, and it is hoped that while the general reader may be informed and entertained, the student of history will find illuminated here for the first time the obscure and shadowy precincts of Rio Grande witch lore.

It was not until the tag end of the nineteenth century that the practice of witchcraft along the Rio Grande began to attract the attention of serious writers and researchers. But since that time a body of witch lore has been made available in copious detail allowing us to examine the content of popular belief and to comment upon the role of supernaturalism as distinct historical and social phenomena among the Hispano and Indian peoples who continue to inhabit the far Southwest.

Certain word usages found in the narrative perhaps demand explanation. The Spanish-speaking people of New Mexico are referred to as Hispanos, in conformity with local terminology, while those of South Texas are generally designated Mexican-Americans, a practice that reveals their status as second or third generation immigrants from Mexico. The more recent term, *Chicano*, while offering a concise generic label, has been avoided since it has meaning only in the context of current Hispanic militancy. "Pueblo" has been capitalized when it refers to the communal Indians of the Rio

Grande but is not when used, as in Spanish, to mean a "town" or "village."

A number of persons generously assisted in the research and final drafting of *Witchcraft in the Southwest*. Dr. Dudley Gordon of the Southwest Museum, Los Angeles, kindly furnished me a copy of an important letter on witch customs by Amado Chaves. Gilberto Benito Córdoba of Abiquiu, New Mexico, and Dr. Alfonso Ortiz of Princeton University and San Juan Pueblo both called my attention to materials I would otherwise have missed. Photographer Bart Durham aided in collecting the illustrations, and Crawford Buell of Santa Fe allowed me to examine documents and newspaper files in his possession. Susie Henderson read the entire manuscript and offered numerous editorial suggestions for its improvement. William Rodgers and Jack Schaefer advised me on several vexing problems, and Natalie Beckman helped with the map. Finally, my friends Frank and Judy Turley unstintingly gave encouragement, and in a hundred ways made lighter the load of this book during the months it was in preparation.

MARC SIMMONS

INTRODUCTION

SEVERAL YEARS AGO I was riding horseback along the Rio Grande below Santa Fe accompanied by a teenage Pueblo boy, the son of an Indian family of long acquaintance. As we approached the foot of a dome-shaped hill, I suggested we climb to the top for a view of the river valley and the mountains beyond, but my companion immediately began to raise a series of, to my mind, trivial objections. Thinking that perhaps the elevation contained a sacred shrine, I asked if the village elders had closed it to trespassers. No, nothing like that, he assured me. It was only that the hill had a reputation for evil, and he preferred to stay clear of such places. Since I had not heard of this before, I announced I was going for a look and, without waiting for his reply, spurred my horse up a dim, rocky trail. A few minutes later I noticed he was reluctantly following.

As I had anticipated the summit presented a superb vista, but I could scarcely concentrate on the landscape while the lad at my side fidgeted in the saddle and cast apprehensive glances over his shoulder. Finally in plaintive appeal, he said, "Let's go now. We have no business here. This is where Mrs. ——— who is a witch turned herself into a coyote. She lives down the street from us and puts spells on people." I was taken aback both by the matter-of-fact directness of his statement and by the realization that a twentieth century high school senior was tormented by fears of the supernatural. But as gently as possible, I admitted the hilltop

1

might not be a safe viewpoint, and we had best be on our way.

Not long afterward, a friend of mine related an experience of his own that again reminded me of the prevalence of belief in witchcraft. Two Hispano acquaintances had been visiting his home in Albuquerque one evening and as darkness gathered outside, both became visibly nervous. At last one of the guests left his chair, went to the large picture window, and drew the drapes. With an audible sigh of relief, he remarked, "You know, it's never wise to leave your curtains open at night. Witches prowl around peeping in windows, and if they catch you unaware, they can do you a lot of harm."

The average Anglo is likely to be startled, just as I initially was, by incidents such as these. Episodes of this nature actually occur infrequently because native believers in sorcery carefully hide their convictions concerning supernatural phenomena, knowing that outsiders regard their views with disdain. Only occasionally, when a relationship has been established with confidence, will they pass some offhand remark revealing the depth of their belief in witches and their fear of the danger posed by black magic.

Certainly fears of witchcraft are far more widespread than appear on the surface, and even where manifestations of occult practice are clearly evident, many unknowledgeable people miss them. As one example, I can cite the readily obvious custom of painting door and window frames of southwestern houses in either blue or turquoise. Newcomers, who often adopt this tradition because it seems a nice decorative touch, are invariably unaware that these colors aid in keeping witches out of the home. Bright blue serves as a protective agent since it is the color of the Virgin Mary, while turquoise is the favored hue of the Indians, bringing good luck and effectively checking the dispersion of evil.

Recently in his weekly newspaper column, Pulitzer Prize-winning Indian novelist N. Scott Momaday noted with candor that his own young daughters are inordinately fond of witch stories and that he himself has "a thing about witches." Recalling personal experiences, he reflected that "There are witches at Jémez Pueblo, and when I lived there I knew of them, sure enough. One night I saw some curious lights away in the distance, small points of light moving erratically about at ground level, and I was told that they were 'witch lights.' I thought: Nonsense; there are some boys running about with flashlights, that is all. And then one of the lights rose slowly and moved like a shooting star across the whole expanse of the sky. I shudder to think of it."[1]

Perhaps an open admission such as this indicates that with the changing times the alluring subject of witchcraft need no longer be condemned out of hand as a matter unworthy of serious consideration. At the very least, supernaturalism along the Rio Grande possesses an intriguing history and has contributed significantly to the folk literature and the lore of the river dwellers. If indeed the hour has come to describe and assess the full scope of southwestern witchcraft, then this book will find an unprejudiced audience and may satisfy the curiosity of those who seek to learn more about a segment of our history heretofore shrouded in mystery.

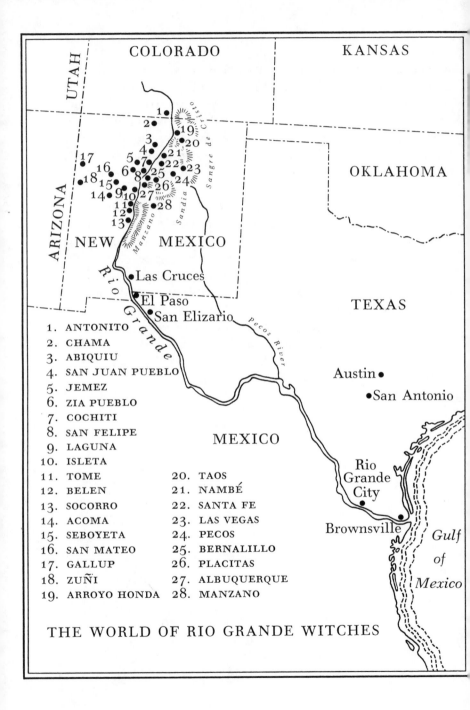

THE WORLD OF RIO GRANDE WITCHES

1. ANTONITO
2. CHAMA
3. ABIQUIU
4. SAN JUAN PUEBLO
5. JEMEZ
6. ZIA PUEBLO
7. COCHITI
8. SAN FELIPE
9. LAGUNA
10. ISLETA
11. TOME
12. BELEN
13. SOCORRO
14. ACOMA
15. SEBOYETA
16. SAN MATEO
17. GALLUP
18. ZUÑI
19. ARROYO HONDA
20. TAOS
21. NAMBÉ
22. SANTA FE
23. LAS VEGAS
24. PECOS
25. BERNALILLO
26. PLACITAS
27. ALBUQUERQUE
28. MANZANO

1

A Dark Heritage

THE STORY OF WITCHCRAFT is almost as old and as wide as human history itself. It may well represent, as one scholar contends, the vestigal remains of a religious complex forming part of a generalized Paleolithic culture that was originally common to all human societies throughout the world.[1] Upon this ancient foundation peoples of every continent and major island developed their own distinctive elaborations, adding customs, rites, and practices that harmonized with their peculiar view of the universe and the supernatural.

Witchcraft does not lend itself to simple definition because, unlike formal religion, it lacks a consistent or standardized body of belief. Moreover, it is closely bound up with the problem of evil and men have always had more difficulty determining, within precise limits, what is bad than what is good. At the most elemental level among primitive peoples, witchcraft assigns meaning to the inexplicable by providing a native theory of failure, misfortune, and death. It is an attempt to interpret the darker aspects of life that chill the souls of men and to explain, albeit through improbable answers, the nature of the vast unknown.

As it evolved in Europe and was later carried to the New World, witchcraft consisted of an amorphous body of magical lore closely tied to Devil worship, fertility rites, fortune telling, hexes and incantations, and problems of health and sickness. For purposes of classification, the craft was divided into degrees. The first, the practice of white magic, provided charms or spells for benevolent purposes. The second degree of witchcraft, black magic, perpetuated evil and was used by persons whose intent was entirely malicious. Finally in the third degree the witch went beyond invoking the aid of the Devil and made an actual compact to become his servant.[2]

Anthropologist Margaret Murray put forward the hypothesis some years ago that the witches of Western Europe were the lingering adherents of a cult forming part of the pagan religion displaced by Christianity.[3] According to her view, when a new religion takes root, the god or gods of the old faith become the Devil of the new. The pre-Christian Old Religion was called Wicca (Craft of the Wise) in England, and from this word derived "witchcraft" and the name for the black arts. Further, Murray believes that the prehistoric god with horns and cloven hoofs depicted in cave paintings throughout Europe may be linked to the Devil of the witch cults. This pagan deity, often pictured as a goat, lustful and lecherous, became the arch symbol of evil for Christians and stood as the antithesis of belief in God. The Devil thus served two functions: he was the source of supernatural power for those dedicated to witchcraft; and, for Christian inquisitors, his existence offered an irrefutable basis for the charge of heresy.[4]

In reality, during the Middle Ages the established Church gave little attention to the pockets of paganism that survived within its midst. Only after the mid-thirteenth century with the establishment of the papal Inquisition did the struggle begin in earnest to eradicate witchcraft, necromancy (communication with the dead), divination, and allied occult arts. The strongest salvo in the new war was launched in 1484 by Pope Innocent VIII, who issued a Bull summoning the nations of Europe to rescue the Christian Church, imperiled by the machinations of witches and Satanists. The tenor of his words was urgent: ". . . many persons of both sexes unmindful of their own salvation and straying from the Catholic Faith have abandoned themselves to devils, incubi, and succubi, and by their incantations, spells, conjurations, and other accursed charms and crafts, enormities and horrid offenses, have slain infants yet in the mother's womb as also the offspring of cattle, and have blasted the produce of the earth."[5] The document codified procedures for bringing witches and other practitioners of evil to justice and appointed inquisitors in every nation, arming them with the apostolic power to convict and punish "in order that criminals so atrocious might no longer pollute the earth."[6] Perhaps nowhere else in history may be found a pronouncement destined to create more panic and bring such suffering upon mankind.

The identification of witches with heretics opened the way for a relentless crusade against all religious nonconformists. Any straying from absolute orthodoxy rendered a person subject to suspicion and during the peak of the witch crazes inevitably led to brutal persecution. The bloody deeds of the self-righteous were justified not only by Innocent's Bull, but also by misinterpretation of the Biblical passage, "Thou shalt not suffer a witch to live" (Exodus 22:18), which seemed to leave no doubt that the crime of witchcraft was a real one under the Mosaic law.

In 1490 two German Dominicans, Henry Kramer and James Sprenger, who enjoyed papal appointments as inquisitors, published *Malleus Maleficarum (The Witches' Hammer)*, laying down a regular form of trial and the course of judicial examination and torture for suspected witches. Stock questions put to victims on the rack included whether they had made a pact and attended midnight meetings with the Devil; whether they participated in the witches' Sabbat; whether they raised whirlwinds and called down the lightning; and whether they had sexual communion with Satan.[7] That such absurdities could be regarded so seriously suggests why for three centuries witch mania found fertile ground in which to flourish.

Once the full power of the Church was unleashed against witchery and heresy, Western Europe became enthralled in an orgy of bloodletting and terror, resembling the primitive cult movements found in every corner of the world. In this case the craze seems to have been part of a general social upheaval attendant upon a period of swift and uncertain change, signaling the end of the Middle Ages, and proving again that old ideas do not surrender their hold upon the mind of man without fierce resistance.

The number of persons put to death as witches from the beginning of the sixteenth century to the height of the panic a hundred years later has been variously estimated by scholars at thirty thousand to several million. Since statistics were not kept, the exact record will never be known, but it is sufficient to state that the total was enormous. Germany won the reputation as the sternest nation, executing thousands as the witch craze gained momentum. In Switzerland during the years 1515 and 1516 five hundred persons were burned as Protestant witches, and in 1524 a thousand suffered death for witchcraft crimes in northern Italy. One inquisitor gleefully claimed credit for destruction of nine hundred witches. Throughout France, where Joan of Arc had been executed as a witch and heretic in 1431, the death pyres consumed prodigious numbers of victims, many of whom had been denounced by their closest relatives. James I of England, obsessed by supernatural phenomena and witches, passed a statute in 1604 making killing by witchcraft a capital offense and providing a year in jail for whoever caused injury through use of charms and spells. The decree resulted in the slaughter of thousands. In Scotland alone thirty-four hundred were burned over a forty-year period for crimes related to witchery. The leading Protestant reformers were as dedicated to the hunt as Catholic bishops and inquisitors and their record stands besmirched with appalling murders. Those inquisitions carried out by John Calvin in 1545 resulted in thirty-one executions for witchcraft in the city of Geneva.

Unfortunately the colonies of the European nations were not immune to the witch dementia that shook the continent. The best known cases are those in New England from 1655 to the end of the century which culminated in the famous trials at Salem. In 1692 several young girls in Salem Village, Massachusetts, began accusing persons of bewitching them, their delusions soon generating a frenzy within the community. An investigating court appointed by the governor became swept up in the madness, and before its work was done nineteen people and two dogs had been sent to the gallows, and an eighty-year-old man had been crushed by weights for refusing to confess.[8]

One aspect of European witchcraft that set it apart from the practice of the black arts elsewhere in the world was the emphasis it placed upon women as the repositories of evil and willing consorts of the Devil. By contrast, the American Indian, as well as most other peoples, was becharmed by as many male as female witches and no special prejudice was heaped upon the latter. Since discrimination against women was firmly rooted in the fabric of Western civilization, it comes as no surprise that in the great epidemic of witch mania they suffered a disproportionate amount of persecution. Certainly much of the sadistic and excessively cruel treatment inflicted upon witches may be taken as a deliberate effort to degrade the female sex. And not all of those harried and tried were ugly, deformed old crones. Many angelic young novices in convents became ensnared in a web of accusations owing solely to deviant but innocent acts of behavior. A young French nun who sat down to supper without saying grace, as a consequence, was charged with swallowing a demon concealed in the leaves of her lettuce salad. Particularly in Germany beautiful maidens were hanged and burned for witchcraft and drawings of voluptuous nude witches were introduced as evidence in trials.[9]

Popular superstition buttressed by ecclesiastical authority attributed much in the realm of evil to Eve and the serpent. The first represented womankind and the second the Devil, and in league they brought misfortune upon man and challenged the supremacy of the Church. An exception was the Virgin Mary, the special enemy of Satan, and it was no coincidence that the Dominican Order, the staunchest defender of the Virgin cult, took the lead in persecuting witches (women "possessed" by the Devil) who were the principal enemies of Mary. Only by hunting out and extirpating hand-maidens of Satan could the world be made safe for the Virgin and the religion established by her Son.[10]

The licentious conduct imputed to witches further illus-trates the nature of the campaign waged to discredit their femininity. At Sabbats, assemblies convened to pay homage to the Devil, they engaged in orgies, gave Satan the "kiss of shame" on his posterior, and submitted to sexual congress with him. While it is true that male witches also partici-pated in these affairs, the overriding stress was always upon women who chose to copulate with the Prince of Hell. In so doing they became the personification of evil and a tower-ing menace to the patriarchal society and religion they had betrayed.

The pattern of witchcraft and persecution in Spain differed somewhat from that of the rest of Europe and must be de-scribed in more detail since the model was carried by colon-ists to the New World and ultimately to the American South-west. The most astonishing fact is that Spain did not succumb to the witch madness that plagued the remainder of the con-tinent. True, a spate of burnings occurred during the first years of the sixteenth century and isolated executions con-tinued for the next three centuries, but throughout, there was a moderation on the part of the authorities not evident in England, Scotland, France, Germany, and other countries.

A minor outbreak of witch frenzy developed in the Prov-ince of Navarre during the late 1520s, but a meeting of in-quisitors decided that the majority of confessions collected were little more than delusions and recommended that min-isters be sent to instruct the ignorant rural peasantry. The secular authorities in Navarre, however, were far less lenient, and certain over-zealous officials instituted mass executions. A high inquisitor went to the province in 1538 with instruc-tions to suppress capital punishment for witchcraft and to inform the population that phenomena such as the blighting of crops and the shrivelling of acorns were caused by the weather rather than witches.[11] Another flare-up in the same area in 1610 resulted in the deaths of five witches at the stake, but after that date comparatively few trials for witch-craft figure in the records of the Inquisition.[12] The last public burning in Spain transpired in 1781 when an old woman was forced to the stake following testimony by witnesses that she had submitted to "carnal converse with the Devil, after which she laid eggs with prophecies written on them."

Throughout the period when the rest of Europe was parad-ing hundreds, even thousands, of condemned persons to the execution square, the Spanish Inquisition loomed as a bul-wark of enlightened reason. Wherever its officers visited rural districts and preached against superstition, accusations of witchcraft immediately subsided. Although obliged to fol-low popular opinion and regard witchery as a crime, au-thorities in practice rejected testimony to such a crime as delusion and Spain was spared the ravages of hysteria so prevalent elsewhere.[13] As is well known, of course, the In-quisition's tolerance did not extend to other forms of heresy, but withal, the numbers of its victims and the cruelty of its methods of torture were manifestly exaggerated in propa-ganda disseminated by Spain's enemies.

In one particular, the thinking of Spaniards coincided with that of their fellow Europeans: the habitual identification of witches as women. A priest, Fray Martín de Castañega, ra-tionalized that this was inevitable since "women are sinks of iniquity." Those aspiring to take up the craft were usually females of low birth or sordid reputation who hoped thereby to improve their economic and social status.[14] In a society where every avenue to opportunity was closed to women of the lower class, resort to the black arts offered a solitary but desperate chance for advancement.

In the sixteenth century, Spanish settlers began pouring into the American colonies and part of their cultural baggage included traditional notions of witchcraft. The earliest conquistadores, firmly grounded in the ideas and legends of the Middle Ages, penetrated the farthest recesses of the New World ever on the lookout for fabled monsters, giants, bearded women, wild men, and dragons.[15] They expected also to find the earthly domicile of the Devil, and in fact sightings of Satan were reported in the Caribbean, Yucatán, and South America. The Maya of Central America believed in a death god, equated by the Spaniards with the Devil, who ruled the underworld and spread evil on the earth. An idol representing him and called Ixchel was shown to the first missionary friars.[16] With the Devil lurking so close at hand, the soldiers of the conquest and the colonists who followed them inevitably perceived demons and witches in their midst since these creatures were necessary in Satan's scheme of malevolent activity.

In witchcraft, as in everything else, the Spaniards imposed their own ideas and patterns of behavior upon the Indian cultures they encountered in America. Yet it is clear that while many traditional details of European witchery were introduced among the native people, belief in the craft itself was aboriginal. Among the Aztecs of Central Mexico, for example, a favorite deity was Tezcatlipoca, lord of the night and patron of the witches. To this god, who possessed supernatural power to change into an animal, human sacrifices were dedicated.[17] Although both male and female witch doctors engaged in magico-medical practices, the majority seem to have been men. The Emperor Montezuma, himself an amateur dabbler in witchcraft, consulted a company of soothsayers when he learned that four-legged monsters with human bodies growing out of their backs (Spaniards on horseback) had landed on the Gulf Coast. Unfortunately these prognosticators foretold of the conquest of the Aztec state by these strange beings, and this prediction was realized within two years in spite of the armies raised and the witchcraft applied by Montezuma.[18]

Aztec witches showed both differences and similarities to their European counterparts. Indian practitioners were ordinarily held in high esteem since they performed black tasks assigned to them by the gods. But witchcraft was always a two-edged weapon and if they fell into disfavor or overplayed their hand, they might be executed. Witches were credited with the power to change themselves into animals, fly through the air, and cause sickness or death, the same capacities attributed to them in Spain. The Aztecs induced illness by drawing blood from a victim, capturing the soul, or introducing worms or pebbles into the body. The more sophisticated Spanish approach entailed jabbing pins into a doll resembling the victim. The most distinctive features of Indian witchery were its lack of organization and its innocuous reputation within society. By contrast Spanish witchcraft was more systematized and complex and was viewed as a grave threat to the maintenance of social order. Witches in Spain reputedly congregated in large bands of one hundred or more members, made up of prostitutes, sexual perverts, and procurers, or they operated in family groups, each generation binding the succeeding one to the Devil's work by bequeathing it the tools of the craft.[19] Other aspects of Spanish practice included the slipping of potions into a victim's food and bewitching him with the evil eye *(mal ojo)*. The latter belief, that a mere gaze can produce the most diabolical evil, existed throughout the Old World and was rapidly picked up by the Indians of Mexico.[20] In sum, witchcraft among the Aztecs, as well as among other tribes, was fairly simple before the Spanish conquest, but in the centuries that followed accretions from European practice transformed it, producing a new and volatile body of supernatural lore.

In spite of the Spaniard's lust for gold and his headlong drive for territorial expansion, it is now recognized that the missionary motive was the most potent and enduring impulse underlying his record of activity in the Americas. Every son of Spain, whether priest, soldier, or settler, felt it incumbent upon himself to assist in bringing the fruits of his nation's Christianity to the unenlightened heathen. The war against native paganism was waged in the name of both the Spanish

Church and the Spanish State, since the two, in the minds of its citizens, were insolubly linked. Where external facets of Indian religion coincided with Catholic practice, the old ways were reworked and handed back to the people in a slightly different guise in an effort to ease and speed the transition to the new cult. In most cases, however, intensive indoctrination was necessary to impress points of unfamiliar theology upon native converts. The haste with which this was done and the stress it placed upon the Indians bore at least one unexpected result: in the wake of the missionary program, witchcraft expanded prodigiously.

Catholic bishops writing to their superiors in the mother country remarked with some frequency upon the fact that the Indians understood little of the religion that was preached to them, and evidence abounded that the formalism and dogma of the Church was being diluted by both ancient superstitions and a proliferation of new ones. In large measure this dilution was traceable to the confusion generated among the aboriginal people by the effort to impose upon them the totally foreign European concept of evil. For the Indians, be they the Aztecs of Mexico or the Pueblos along the Rio Grande, a strict division of the universe into opposing forces of good and evil was incomprehensible. They viewed evil as a shadowy negative force present to some degree in every man and god and an immutable part of life one simply endured. That the new priests placed such emphasis upon evil and that their creed looked toward its total elimination was a matter evoking astonishment and dismay.

The earliest Spanish chronicles describe the numerous idols and deities in the Indian pantheon as demons in league with the Devil, and traditional witches as his allies and enemies of the Church. This preoccupation with sin, evil-mongering, idolatry, and witchery soon infected the impressionable Indians and they too became engrossed in the contemplation of iniquity and the black side of supernaturalism. From here it was but a short step to an obsession with witchcraft. An anthropologist has described the process succinctly in these

terms: "The padres encouraged witchcraft beliefs by stig-
matizing as witchcraft what they disapproved of. The unbap-
tized became witches; all who practice non-Christian rites
are wizards. Witchcraft was the nearest approach to the
Catholic conception of sin that was made by the Indians and
the padres took advantage of it."[21]

The roots that witchery sunk in the Mexican soil in the
sixteenth century took firm hold and flourish to this day.
Witchcraft *(brujería)*, sorcery *(hechicería)*, the evil eye
(mal ojo), and other forms of occultism have become integral
parts of the folk culture of the Mexican nation, thriving in
rural hamlet and city alike. Contemporary witches and sorcerers prepare love potions and cause or cure illness by resorting to one of the craft's three forms — red, white, and
black. Red is for bewitching, white for healing, and black for
death.[22] In both Indian and mestizo communities, spells are
cast upon those who violate the accepted rules of good conduct or who antagonize a witch. To be safe from witchcraft
it is essential to give offense to no one, to avoid amassing
more wealth than one's neighbors, and to conform in all
details to the norms established by common consent.

Throughout Mexico certain villages suffer even yet from
a reputation of being centers for witchcraft. As will be demonstrated later, the same held true until fairly recent times
for several Indian and Mexican-American towns north of
the Rio Grande. What becomes apparent is that, even allowing for regional variations, a fairly uniform pattern of witchcraft belief arose wherever the colonial Spaniards settled in
North America and that such belief persists to the present
day, sometimes weak and at other times strong, but remaining as a curious anomaly — a relic of the darker age of man,
still breathing life in the twentieth century.

2

The Devil's Domain on the Rio Grande

THE RANKS OF HELMETED CONQUISTADORES and sandal-shod padres penetrating Mexico's vast northern frontier after 1540 found, if not golden cities and monsters, at least enough marvels to provoke wonder. Incredibly immense herds of vicious, woolly cattle, or *cíbola* as the Spaniards called bison, roamed the expansive plains of Texas. In the lush valleys of the southern Rockies, elk, referred to by the newcomers as "sorrel deer," browsed on mountain mahogany and scrub oak, and on the higher timbered slopes the largest and most deadly animal on the continent—the grizzly bear—reigned without fear of challenge. Vast deserts, containing stretches of sand dunes as desolate as the Sahara, and bubbling hot springs emitting sulphurous vapors like the chimneys of hell met and awed the first Spanish explorers. López de Cárdenas, one of Coronado's captains and the first European to visit what is now northern Arizona, reached the brink of the Grand Canyon and gazed in stupefaction at the greatest abyss in the crust of the earth. His amazement in confronting a boundless landscape was shared by other Spaniards who made the initial entry onto the Great Plains and discovered that in an ocean of grass without landmarks they were as disoriented and apprehensive as sailors adrift at sea.

But it was the native people — the reddish-dun colored inhabitants of plain, mesa, and river valley — that aroused the most interest among the wayfaring Europeans. Some of the nomadic buffalo-hunting tribesmen adorned themselves

16

with elaborate tattoos. Other Indians on the lower Rio Grande were veritable cannibals, roasting victims barbecue fashion for the feast. On the upper part of the same river dwelled a populous and astonishingly advanced people, comfortably ensconced in multi-storied apartment houses of adobe or stone masonry, and named by the earliest Spaniards, the Pueblos, meaning "Townsmen." Upon these Indians, colonial administrators, soldiers, and priests fastened their attention and among them laid the first foundations of Western society in the far Southwest.

The Pueblos at once aroused admiration, as much for their productive farming, fine ceramics and weaving, and docility of nature as for their distinctive architecture. But upon one aspect of their culture — religion — the Spaniards understandably looked with undisguised abhorrence and disgust. Pueblo religious practice, replete with supplications to multiple deities, masked ceremonials, and snake dances, bore the clear stamp of wizardry, and the tonsured Christian fathers with pious solemnity pronounced the entire native ecclesiastical structure a creation of Satan. Hernán Gallegos, chronicler of the Chamuscado-Rodríguez expedition of 1581, summed up the prevailing view with a brief description of a ritual he witnessed at one of the Rio Grande villages. A dancing medicine man, bathed in blood from whip lashes delivered by his companions, conversed with a large rattlesnake "as thick as an arm" and received from it messages that only he could understand. With disarming simplicity Gallegos commented, "We thought this snake might be the Devil, who has them enslaved. For this reason God our Lord willed that the settlement and its idolatrous people should be discovered, in order that they might come to the true faith."[1] Taken in this light, the manifest mission of the Spanish padres, as they saw it, was one of breaking the chains imposed by the Devil, freeing the benighted Pueblos from supernatural slavery, and eradicating all forms of native religious practice which, with self-professed authority, they stigmatized as witchcraft.

In 1598, Juan de Oñate, scion of a wealthy north Mexican mining family, undertook the settlement and organization of the province of New Mexico in the heart of the Pueblo country, and twelve years later colonists established Santa Fe as their capital. From the beginning, Franciscan fathers fanned out through the several score Indian communities to build missions, create schools and workshops, and preach against native ways of religion. Fray Alonso de Benavides, author of a detailed report on the missionary effort in New Mexico, characterized the entire Pueblo male population as divided between warriors and sorcerers, the latter term referring to the large number of medicine men present in every village. These sorcerers, he explained, held their superstitious clansmen under their sway by arrogating to themselves the power to make the rain fall, the earth yield crops, and even to form the clouds and paint them with a sunset. Benavides, with smug satisfaction, recorded that "from the house of one old Indian sorcerer I once took out more than a thousand idols of wood, painted in the fashion of a game of nine pins, and I burned them in the public plaza."[2]

In his discourse on sorcery appears a description of women evidently addicted to witchcraft. A certain class of females, grown fat and lustful, connived with the Devil and resorted to idolatry to gain the attention of men. Women who wished that men should desire them, Benavides says, went out into the countryside plump and well-fed and on a small hill set up a stone shrine or pole around which they scattered sacred cornmeal. For eight days they fasted, swallowed emetic herbs, and flogged themselves with whips, and when at last they returned to the pueblo, their bodies drawn lean and their faces pinched like that of a demon, they were full of confidence that the first man they might see would succumb to their charms and present them rich gifts of cotton blankets.

Witches also played an active role in opposing the work of the Christian teachers, since this was part of their function as instruments of Satan. From a fellow missionary, Father Benavides learned of an incident at Taos Pueblo in which an old Indian woman, committed to witchery, had labored to discredit the practice of monogamy introduced by the Spanish priest. Under the pretext of going into the mountains for firewood, the witch lured four Taos women away from the village and attempted to persuade them that the old system — a man taking multiple wives — was superior to the foreign one they had adopted after baptism. As the party was returning to the pueblo, Benavides relates with perfect faith that "the witch not ceasing from her sermon and the heavens being clear and serene, a thunderbolt fell and slew that infernal mistress of the Demon, right between the good Christians who were resisting her evil doctrine. Directly all the pueblo flocked thither; and seeing that rap from heaven, all those who were living in secret concubinage got married."[3] Such an episode, of course, confirmed the fathers in the belief that their battle with the minions of the Devil was a real and physical one.

While a legion of missionaries was striving to root out sorcery among the Pueblo Indians and banish Satan and his helpers from the shores of the Rio Grande, Spanish colonists in Santa Fe and in the dozen or more small ranching communities spread across the new province were finding their own lives bedeviled by contagious fears of witches and assorted supernatural forces. That we possess a considerable body of detail concerning superstition and witchcraft from the remote period of the 1600s is due largely to the fact that these aberrations fell under the jurisdiction of the Holy Office of the Inquisition which kept voluminous records of its investigatory activities and judicial trials. No court of the Inquisition was ever established in the Southwest, but the chief missionary friar serving there received a special commission from the principal tribunal in Mexico City, allowing him to gather evidence and imprison persons charged with heresy, apostasy, witchcraft, and other religious crimes, and refer those cases that warranted prosecution to the main body in the viceregal capital.

A typical case from the files of the Holy Office concerned

an unlettered cowboy, Luís de Rivera, who was moved by the blandishments of a sorcerer to make a pact with the Devil. As a youth Rivera had immigrated from his native Spain to the cattle country of Chihuahua and while working as a stock herder had been led into dark paths. First, an Indian revealed to him the secrets of herbal magic, particularly the use of a plant which possessed the power of attracting women and causing them to submit to carnal relations. Then the young man met a Negro slave who introduced him to the lore of demonology and showed him how to win the favor of the Devil by which he gained supernatural aid in rounding up cattle and in catching a mustang on foot. As a mark of his alliance with evil, the Negro had a figure of Satan tattooed on the sole of his foot and he carried a book on the pages of which he had painted crude pictures of demons. He offered to sell the volume to Rivera, explaining that if he would draw blood from his nose and with it sign his name at the bottom of the pictures, thus concluding a pact with the Devil and selling his soul, the ruler of hell would always lend him assistance. Childlike, Rivera accepted the offer, paid a peso and a half for the book, drew blood, and signed his name. But within a week he became fearful that his thoughless action might involve serious sin, and he tore up his pictorial contract. Yet during the years that followed, his secret indiscretion weighed heavily on his conscience and the Devil never ceased to torment his soul.

In 1628 demon-plagued Luís de Rivera signed on as a mule drover with a supply caravan going north to New Mexico. He hoped that perhaps a change of country would allow him to forget the fears that eroded his will and provide a reversal of his bad fortune. Unhappily, however, the wagon train in the midst of its journey experienced a mule and cattle stampede resulting in serious loss. The drivers and stock handlers, a superstitious lot, speculated that a confederate of the Devil must be among them, for only he could have caused the ruinous stampede. In the face of such talk, poor Rivera's self-control was shattered, and thoroughly repentant he confessed his terrible secret to one of the friars in the caravan. With arrival in Santa Fe, the priest denounced him before the Inquisition's representative, and he was arrested and hustled off to Mexico City in irons. At his trial, Rivera, who readily confessed his guilt, threw himself on the mercy of the ecclesiastical court and pleaded that his acts had been the result of youthful ignorance, not of conscious intent to sin or cut himself off from the Church. The tribunal, after lengthy review of all evidence, concluded that this was the essential truth of the matter, and it let the contrite cowboy off with an astonishingly mild penance. In most instances, as is well known, the Inquisition gave little heed to abjurations and mercy pleas, condemning the guilty to long prison terms or even the stake.[4]

In the early 1630s, the agent of the Holy Office in Santa Fe began looking into a growing series of charges that residents of the New Mexican capital were yielding to a wide variety of superstitious practices and that many actually played about with black magic, crossing the limits of orthodoxy and entering the dark realm of witchcraft. According to dozens of sworn depositions taken by church officials, a shocking number of soldiers in the royal garrison were unfaithful to their wives, and the aggrieved ladies, in a desperate bid to win back the affection of their husbands, were casting about for love potions or magic philters. Most of the formulas for these derived from Mexican Indian servants attached to the majority of Spanish households, and the mixtures being handed about and slipped into morning breakfast cups included such ingredients as herbs, powders, cornmeal, milk, fried or mashed worms — and urine, either of the defecting husband or of his mistress. The purpose of these concoctions was simply to win back the man's devotion, or at the very least cause him to lose interest in his outside love. All who resorted to occult artifices of this nature left themselve open to censure and even criminal prosecution by the Inquisition court. Yet the traffic in amorous potions continued, for spurned wives cared more for the restoration of domestic tranquility and the fidelity of their husbands than they did for the strict rules of the Church.[5]

Of far graver nature than the commerce in love charms were the charges of witchcraft leveled by several Spanish citizens against two women, Beatriz de los Angeles, a Mexican Indian of known intelligence, and her half-breed daughter, Juana de la Cruz. Rumor attributed several deaths to Beatriz's diabolical powers and much of the Santa Fe community lived in fear of displeasing her. In order to try out one of her evil potions, she experimented on two Indian servants, and they both died. When one of her lovers, Diego Bellido, started a quarrel and beat her, she fed him a bowl of bewitched corn gruel. He shortly fell ill with violent intestinal pains and passed away after several weeks of agony. Hernando Márquez, a royal officer, died after Beatriz placed a hex on him for sleeping with her daughter — this according to his brother Pedro. A servant in the witch's household reported that her mistress made small idols of people she intended to harm and buried them under the hearth. Another witness claimed to have found a miniature figurine of one of the victims hanging from a tree on land belonging to Beatriz.

A trove of improbable stories also gathered around the head of the daughter, Juana. Many of her alleged activities bore the earmarks of the classic witchcraft pattern. She killed her unfaithful husband by giving him a cup of enchanted milk. Possessed of the evil eye, she gazed on children and made them ill. One such infant died, while another was saved by being smoked with a burned bit of Juana's clothing. The malevolent eye turned upon a third child caused a firemark *(arestín)* to appear on its face. Finally, popular belief attributed to Juana the ability to fly about at night and spy on her paramours to see if they remained faithful. These winged excursions were made, not on the traditional broom, but inside an egg.[6]

These and other stories were presented to Father Esteban de Perea, official of the Inquisition, as evidence that the two women were confirmed and practicing witches. It speaks well of the priest that, like many of his contemporaries in Spain, he was not moved by wild accusations or mass delusions. After a careful investigation, he concluded that the complaints against the women were maliciously motivated or were the result of fabrications by ignorant busy-bodies and he ordered the case closed. The suspects were indeed fortunate to receive official clearance, for at other times in New Mexico accused witches fell victim to the anger of their neighbors before authorities could intervene and set matters straight.

The most extraordinary instance of witchcraft during the seventeenth century involved a German trader, Bernardo Gruber, who came to the New Mexican settlements from Sonora in 1668 with a pack train. His mules bore fine stockings, gloves, embroidered cloth, buckskins, and iron tools and weapons. Apparently he was accustomed to roam the Apache-infested frontier seeking customers and must have been endowed with an exceptional amount of business enterprise and courage. Unfortunately the circumstances that cast him in this curious role and originally led him from his native land are not known. The Spanish records tell us only of his arrest on charges of sorcery and of his subsequent death.

Gruber's troubles began when several Pueblo Indians denounced him before their priest, claiming that he had shared a devilish secret with them and instructed them in bizarre supernatural practices. One of the informants testified that "the man named Bernardo Gruber, whom they call 'the German,' had told him that in his country they make certain writings on the first day of the feast of the Nativity during the time when the Gospel is being intoned, and that if a person eats one of these writings, he becomes so strong that for the space of twenty-four hours after having eaten the said paper, he cannot be injured by any sword or bullet whatsoever."

Another witness asserted that Gruber "had given him a paper with some words and characters on it, and told him that if he would eat the paper neither the arrows of the Apaches, nor bullets, nor swords, would wound him. He said it was customary in his nation, Germany, to use this paper when they went to war. This Bernardo tried out the paper on an Indian boy of Las Salinas, who, although they struck him with a knife, was not wounded." Juan Nieto, a native of the same place, declared he had gotten hold of one of the mysterious papers, had eaten it, and then tried to injure himself with a dagger. After his wife snatched it away, he pricked his body with a knife and an awl without drawing blood or feeling any pain.

These and similar damaging statements were sufficient to cause the chief Franciscan prelate to begin looking more closely into the strange German's activities. He found that a veritable throng of Indians had been introduced to the magical papers, some even inside the missions while Mass was in progress. When Gruber was summoned to give his version of the affair, he unabashedly acknowledged possession of a powerful formula that conveyed invulnerability. At the insistence of the priest, he wrote his esoteric recipe on the wall in this form:

† A. B. N. A. † A. D. N. A. †

It is little wonder that the revelation resulted in his arrest on charges of sorcery. Among European witch cults, a spell or incantation was often written down to be eaten or repeated by the user. One spell designed to cure toothache entailed repetition of the words "Galbus, Galbat, Galdes, Galdat."[7] Another cabalistic formula, effective in conjuring up the Devil, went as follows:

Bagabi laca bachabe
Lamac cahi achababe
Karrelyos.[8]

Gruber affirmed that his own knowledge of the supernatural had been gained in his native country where verbal prescriptions such as these were commonly employed by the poorer folk. Quite likely he was ignorant of the fact that use of his

simple-minded spell was classed as a religious crime in the
Spanish colonies, but he was not long in learning the nature
of the law. Clamped in irons, he was imprisoned at the
Pueblo mission of Abó to await transfer to the jails of the
Inquisition in Mexico City.

In some manner the German communicated with his Indian servants who had accompanied him from Sonora, and
in the middle of the night they managed to pry loose the bars
of his cell and permit his escape. Although freed from the
clutches of the Inquisition, Gruber's good fortune was short-
lived. A few weeks later, Captain Andrés de Peralta, leading
a small patrol along a desert road in southern New Mexico,
reported finding "a roan horse tied to a tree by a halter. It
was dead, and near it was a doublet or coat of blue cloth
lined with otter-skin. There were also a pair of trousers of the
same material, and other remnants of clothing that had de-
cayed. I examined them, and as it seemed that they belonged
to Bernardo Gruber, the fugitive, I made a search which did
not result in vain, for I found at once all of his hair and the
remnants of the clothing which he had worn. I and my companions searched carefully for the bones, and found in very
widely separated places the skull, three ribs, two long bones,
and two other little bones which had been gnawed by animals. It is supposed that Indians traveling with the German
killed him. . . ." Lamentably for Bernardo Gruber, the scraps
of paper that originally led to his predicament had failed to
offer him any protection from his enemies, and, as it did with
many a person who resorted to sorcery, the supernatural
power he toyed with finally turned against him.[9]

In the years after 1650, the Spanish friars grew increas-
ingly intolerant of the Pueblo medicine men and heaped
abuses upon them, claiming that they perniciously obstructed
the missionary program through the application of black
magic and hexing of the padres. The work of conversion was,
in fact, proceeding at a dismally slow pace, and the missionaries, to alleviate their own sense of failure, stepped up the

persecution of native priests. With assistance of royal troops, they periodically raided the Pueblo religious chambers, or kivas, confiscating ceremonial paraphernalia and carting it into the village plaza for public burning. Infuriated over these acts, the medicine men labored all the harder to guide their people away from the preaching of the fathers, and this in turn brought sterner punishment upon their heads.

For several decades the Spaniards flogged, imprisoned, condemned to slavery, or even executed Pueblo leaders in a futile effort to stamp out the last vestiges of paganism and witchcraft. Matters reached a crisis in 1675 when four Indians were hanged, forty-seven whipped and enslaved, and others jailed for killing several missionaries and bewitching a church inspector, Father Andrés Durán. The verdict read that all were guilty of sorcery and of communion with the Devil as well as of plotting with neighboring Apaches to rebel against the government.

A large delegation of chiefs and warriors appeared in Santa Fe and confronted the Spanish governor, demanding release of their sorcerers and offering as ransom chickens, eggs, tobacco, beans, and bales of hides. The governor was much taken aback by the show of force and he hastened to comply with their request by freeing the prisoners. But his retreat in the face of this threat simply demonstrated that the Spanish hold on the province was fast deteriorating.[10]

One of the medicine men who suffered humiliation at the whipping post in 1675 was a native of San Juan Pueblo known as Popé. From the moment of his release, he vowed vengeance against the sons of the conquerors, and for the next five years he strove tirelessly using every natural and supernatural power at his disposal to forge an alliance among all the Pueblos against the common enemy. Craftily, he appealed both to popular superstition and Indian patriotism and asserted his authority to leadership by claiming to be the personal spokesman and representative of *El Demonio*, the Spaniard's "Devil." At Taos Popé established his headquarters and led strange diabolical rites in the underground kiva, where according to rumor he communed with Satan and conspired to bring the hated oppressors of the Indians to their knees. According to one widely-believed story he traveled from one village to another on a whirlwind, in the best tradition of flying witches, to cement the unity necessary for victory.

The fatal blow fell on the morning of August 10, 1680. Along the cottonwood shaded banks of the Rio Grande, on the Pecos and Galisteo Rivers to the east, and in the deserts of the west, the Pueblos rose en masse and slew colonists, friars, soldiers, and government officials. The grim toll amounted to twenty-one priests and over four hundred settlers dead, with the entire Spanish province a smoldering ruin. Many persons in the south were able to escape the warriors' fury and flee to El Paso, as did some twenty-five hundred survivors who rallied in Santa Fe and fought their way out of the capital. The disaster was of such magnitude, the greatest loss ever sustained by Spain in her overseas empire, that official reports could account for it only through the intervention of the Devil and his legion of sorcerers on the side of the Indians. Although it is now clear that monumental ineptitude on the part of Spanish officials and missionaries was the direct cause of the tragedy, it is safe to conclude that delusions concerning the role of sorcery and the application of witchcraft so distracted the Spaniards that they failed to perceive more fundamental causes of native unrest, and that this failure indirectly contributed to the debacle. In any event, if Satan did have a hand in the bloody event, as both parties so firmly believed, it surely must have been his greatest triumph.[11]

For twelve years the Pueblos held fast to their independence, but in the period 1692–93 an army of reconquest under General Diego de Vargas entered the province, fought a series of costly battles, and established Spain's dominion anew along the upper Rio Grande. The Franciscans reopened their missions, but much chastened by the fateful loss of 1680, their sermons were no longer shrill, nor were their denunciations of medicine men as sorcerers so strident. In fact they felt content to leave Indian dances and rituals alone as long as they were kept discreetly in the background and the Pueblos paid nominal lip service to the outward forms of Christian practice.

After 1700 a steady stream of new settlers moved into the area from Mexico, and the province grew both in population and economic prosperity. Santa Fe had been refounded by De Vargas; other towns soon appeared at Santa Cruz, Bernalillo, Albuquerque, and elsewhere; and hardy colonists moved into the countryside to build farms and haciendas. But among this new generation of Spanish pioneers as well as among the Pueblo Indians, belief in witchcraft still held powerful sway.

Historian Adolph Bandelier, surveying the Spanish colonial archives in Santa Fe during the 1880s, noted the presence of dozens of papers relating to witchcraft cases, mostly from the eighteenth and early nineteenth centuries. Many of these documents have since disappeared, but those remaining reveal much concerning prevailing notions of witch lore and the practice of demonology. The sampling of cases that follows shows that problems growing out of superstitious belief were abiding ones, and that a folk society, such as that on the Rio Grande, was strongly conformist and suspicious of any member whose deviant behavior suggested association with the black arts.

The Bewitchment of Doña Leonor, 1708

Doña Leonor Domínguez, wife of Miguel Martín and a resident of Santa Fe, petitioned the Spanish governor to conduct a formal investigation into the causes that resulted in her bewitchment: "Being extremely ill with various troubles and maladies which seemed to be caused by witchcraft, . . . and although I am a Catholic Christian by the goodness of God, I know that there have been many examples in this Province of persons of my sex who have been hexed by devilish art, including, as is well known, Augustina Romero, Ana María, wife of Luiz López, and María Lujan, my sister-in-law. Therefore I beg that Your Excellency may be pleased to send one of your agents to my house to take my legal declaration and solemn oath of what passed between me and three Indian women of the Pueblo of San Juan whom I suspect as witches. And I promise to declare the reasons for my suspicion, and your agent may observe the condition in which I find myself, which is a matter of public knowledge and notoriety."

The governor evidently decided that enough truth resided in Doña Leonor's complaint to warrant a judicial inquiry and he dispatched a magistrate to her home. This official found the afflicted woman bedridden, so ill and weak that she could hardly express herself, and from all appearances on the point of death. She testified under oath and the sign of the cross that on the previous Holy Thursday while attending Mass at the town of Santa Cruz, she observed three women of San Juan sitting near her, and that they cast mysterious glances upon her and whispered in a strange manner among themselves. She was immediately filled with terror, which increased when one of the witches approached and laid a hand on her back. At first she thought the woman intended to steal the buttons from her cloak, but shortly she began to itch and then to feel a profound sickness, and by this knew that she had fallen victim to a spell. For this reason she wished to prefer charges against her oppressors.

Next the magistrate traveled twelve leagues north of Santa Fe to the village of San Juan where he arrested the alleged witches and began their interrogation through interpreters. All three hotly denied any working of black magic against Doña Leonor, but in the course of their remarks it was revealed that one of the women had been her husband's concubine years before, and that another was recently accused by Doña Leonor of trifling with her spouse's affections. An additional sinister detail was added when the investigator learned that following the Holy Thursday Mass at Santa Cruz, Leonor confronted her husband in the churchyard, passed some remarks concerning his infidelity, and slapped him.

Now that an amorous triangle beclouded the issue, more affidavits were taken and Doña Leonor again underwent questioning from her sickbed. Asked if her assumptions about the evil of the Indians were made because they had a public reputation as witches, she disclaimed any knowledge of previous acts of witchcraft on their part. But she maintained that San Juan was reputed to be filled with witches and hence she had drawn her own conclusions. The flimsy nature and insincerity of her original accusations became more apparent when Doña Leonor admitted harboring suspicions that her husband had been intimate with one or more of the now imprisoned ladies.

The governor, as chief judicial officer of the province, reviewed the assembled declarations and testimony, and pronounced his verdict, wisely decreeing that the charge of witchcraft "is false, futile, and despicable, by reason of which and of the good effects resulting from the said proceedings, I must declare, as I do, the three Indian women to be free as regards the matter produced in this case." The legal doings had consumed more than two weeks, but there is no doubt that justice was done.[12]

Isleta Witches, 1733

Bicente García and his wife, Spanish citizens residing near the Pueblo of Isleta on the Rio Grande, complained to their alcalde ("district judge") that they were both seriously ill as a result of the evil eye and a witchcraft spell cast upon them by the Indian Melchor Trujillo. The alcalde initiated hearings and took statements from a variety of witnesses. One of these, Joseph Reaño, averred that he saw Trujillo give the García couple a drink, and soon after they were forced to bed and seemed to die. Then suddenly they revived from the dead, a miracle beyond the words of the witness to describe. Further investigation revealed that the enchanted drink contained peyote, a cactuslike plant that produces a narcotic effect.

El Casique, the chief of Isleta, was called before the alcalde and questioned about the affair. He disclosed that Melchor Trujillo was a curer rather than a sorcerer and had in fact been attempting to heal the Garcías from hexes placed upon them by other witches. And just who were these "other witches"? El Casique named several Isletans, men and women, and then blandly announced that he was the head of their occult fraternity and held responsibility for placing spells on several leading Spaniards, including the local priest, Fray Antonio Miranda. The alcalde, astounded by this casual statement, inquired how the bewitching had been accomplished. From a magical stone, he was informed, the witches rubbed off dust and annointed themselves, and El Casique, wearing special robes and aided by his helper, El Flaco, led the others in an evil ritual during which they pierced dolls resembling their victims with pins.

All persons named by the chief as his accomplices in sorcery received a summons to appear for examination, and each confirmed in a general way what he had said. Under pressure from the judge, they surrendered to the court various dolls and other offensive objects. El Flaco, for instance, turned over four small idols or dolls and a string adorned with three beads. Getting El Casique to give up his collection of charms proved to be more difficult, however. The alcalde went to his home to confiscate nine dolls supposedly hidden in a corn bin, and there recorded that "El Casique turned over to me a small oblong rock, pink in color and very smooth in texture. Then he turned over a buckskin bag containing a white rock wrapped in a small cloth as well as some of the idols." But the remaining dolls were not lodged in the corn bin and the defendant obstinately refused to divulge their whereabouts.

Resuming his questioning of the other parties, the magistrate learned that they had been led into the wayward path of black magic by El Casique, that they followed his directions explicitly, and that he exercised full control over their lives. Under cross-examination, the chief denied none of this. Finally the alcalde ordered him strung up by his hands with a rope and when he still proved unwilling to disclose the whereabouts of the missing dolls, ten lashes were laid on his back. At this point El Casique confessed that he really wanted to tell the truth, but that the Devil held him in bondage and would not permit him to do so.

The alcalde then reported, "Realizing the obstacles I was facing, I called upon the Father Minister so that he might get him to confess, and again this was of no avail, but instead El Casique, playing a small deception on me, gave me a bag with a white rock and said this was an idol, and so he took up my time the whole day." In exasperation, the judge suspended his investigation, and, concluding that the ten whip lashes constituted punishment enough, announced he wished to hear no more of witchcraft.[13]

Mysterious Death of a Priest, 1766

When Father Félix Ordoñez y Machado, minister of the Abiquiu mission, died from unexplained causes, an Indian girl denounced a certain man and his wife as responsible for causing his demise through witchcraft. The chief magistrate of the district, Don Carlos Fernández, arrested the accused as well as several other suspicious persons and conveyed them to the town of Santa Cruz for trial. The record of the ensuing proceedings is said to have amounted to more than a hundred pages, but unfortunately this document has been lost. All we know is that the defendants were found guilty of contributing to the priest's passing by resort to supernatural devices and were condemned to a period of servitude in the households of Christians. In addition, royal troops were dispatched to Abiquiu, located in the mountains west of the Rio Grande, to destroy relics of witchcraft, including a stone with diabolical inscriptions.[14]

An Execution at Sandía Pueblo, 1796

In the summer of 1797 Spanish officials began to hear rumors that a Sandía Indian named Cristóbal had been tried for witchcraft during the previous year inside the pueblo and had perished as a result of ill treatment. By quiet inquiry, several native witnesses were found who gave details of the unfortunate affair. The village governor Juan Domingo and the war chief Diego Antonio had called the Indian populace to assemble in the ceremonial kiva and there proclaimed that one of their own number, Cristóbal, was a fiendish sorcerer. According to their evidence, he had employed black magic to assist a war party of Apaches in running off some of the town's livestock to get revenge for an imagined slight.

Under direction of Pueblo officers, the culprit's feet were placed in a pair of stocks and his hands tied with a rope from a horse halter. Then his arms were drawn up and he was suspended from a roof beam of the kiva. After receiving eighteen or twenty lashes, the suffering Cristóbal confessed to being a witch; the beating forthwith continued, and he died.

No more than this could be learned. The few persons who gave the first reports experienced immediate reprisals at the hands of their fellow tribesmen, and civil investigators could find no one else willing to testify. Governor Fernando de Chacón in Santa Fe read the preliminary reports and concluded that evidence was too thin to warrant further action. Moreover, the subject of witchcraft was always an emotional and touchy one, and at least in this instance not worth stirring up the Indians, so he ordered the matter dropped.[15]

Father Barreras Reprimanded, 1799

The minister of the mission of San Ildefonso Pueblo, Fray Antonio Barreras, fell ill. He traced his adversity to a spell laid upon him by three Indians, Juan Domingo Caracho, Joseph Antonio Paez, and a woman herb doctor, María Varguer Lucero. All were dangerous enchanters (*maleficiadores*) in his view, and he applied to the local alcalde, Don Manuel García de la Mora, for assistance. Now, it was the alcalde's duty under the law to press formal charges and conduct a trial if a genuine case of witchcraft was involved. Instead of following this procedure, García de la Mora arrested the two accused men and calmly handed them over to the disposition of the priest, along with a pillory used in the punishment of criminals. Father Barreras, a man of little prudence and violent temper, undertook in his own way to prove that the pair had bewitched him and caused his illness, and when he subjected them to torture, Caracho died as a result of physical abuse.

Such a grave incident was not long in reaching the notice of the governor, and that officer was so appalled by this miscarriage of justice that he felt compelled to inform his superior in Chihuahua, the Commandant General, of the circumstances in the case and ask for guidance. The Commandant consulted his legal advisor and responded with a decree imposing the following penalties upon the parties in the affair: Alcalde García de la Mora, for failing to uphold his office and defend the jurisdiction of the civil court in a case of witchcraft, was deprived of the right to hold any public office for a period of eight years. Father Barreras was removed from his mission station and permanently exiled from the Province of New Mexico, for as the Commandant noted, "He who indulges in capricious acts of this kind, can be of no use to the Church's service." And finally, since evidence indicated that Paez and María Lucero had indeed been guilty of practicing witchcraft, the former was sentenced to four years at hard labor in ankle-chains at the Hacienda de Encinallas, a government sweat-shop in Chihuahua, and the woman was condemned to four years of personal servitude with a Christian family, so that she might learn the rudiments of proper religion.[16]

The Flight of Father Canales, 1800

The first year of the nineteenth century was anything but auspicious for Fray Jaime Canales stationed at Picurís Pueblo. A terrible pain gnawed at his vital organs and the uncertainty over the source of his ailment filled him with anxiety. Although he knew of none of his native parishioners who held a grudge against him, yet he felt that in some manner he had incurred the enmity of a witch and was reaping the bitter fruit of that misstep. Repeatedly he petitioned the

Spanish governor for release from his position and for a travel permit that would allow him to return to the Franciscan chapter house in Mexico City. Only in flight, ran his appeal, was there a chance to escape his devilish tormentor and save his life.

The governor, while remaining highly skeptical that the priest's infirmity was a product of witchcraft, nevertheless recognized that the poor man's fears had rendered him unfit to fulfill his duties. So, sympathizing with his condition, he issued the appropriate license, and Fray Jaime departed from the Rio Grande in haste, seeking refuge from the mysterious forces that had assailed him at Picurís.[17]

These representative cases of witchcraft from the later colonial period demonstrate, first, that in the minds of settlers and clergy the Pueblo Indians, just as in the years prior to 1680, still harbored a preponderant number of sorcerers, and that they posed a continuing threat to the Hispanic community. However, the provincial government by its strong insistence upon adherence to proper legal forms in the investigation, trial, and punishment of witches served as a moderating influence, and doubtless prevented the development of a serious witch craze of the kind that brought misery to so many hapless persons in Europe and New England.

Secondly, these accounts show the degree to which Spain's missionaries on the frontier were ridden by superstition and plagued by fears of bewitchment. Unquestionably, their delusions promoted social discord, encouraged disquietude among gullible laymen, and helped spread rather than stamp out absurd notions associated with witch lore and the Devil's cult. Notwithstanding, it remains probable that only a minority of the priesthood succumbed to a phobia of sorcerers, at least to the extent that legal action became necessary. Certainly its record in the far Southwest, while not spotless, was far cleaner with respect to the persecution of witches than that of many clergymen elsewhere in the Western World.

3

Executions and the Diabolical Kiss

AT THE CONCLUSION of the Mexican War in 1848 most of what is now the southwestern United States passed under American sovereignty. North of the new frontier, extending from the mouth of the Rio Grande to the Pacific shore, thousands of Indians and Mexicans found themselves suddenly subjected to a new political rule and exposed to an aggressive, alien culture that held little respect for their simple folkways. One of the first things to become apparent was that Anglo-Americans had practically no faith in the rites of witchcraft and that sorcery was not a crime under the new law. Williams W. H. Davis, United States Attorney in the new territories, roundly condemned the alleged evidence of witchery he found on every hand. "As evidence of the superstition of the people," he wrote, "I need only mention their general belief in witchcraft and every kind of sorcery, which is not confined alone to the most ignorant portion of the community. In the year 1853 a man was arrested in Taos for this imagined offense, and bound over by an alcalde to answer at the next term of the District Court. When the case came up for trial it was at once dismissed, and the prosecutor was made to understand that there were no such offenses under our laws."[1]

The confusion was perhaps natural since both townsmen and rural folk for two hundred years had been accustomed to haul witchcraft complaints before representatives of the Spanish or Mexican government. Several decades elapsed, in

36

fact, before the new citizens fully understood that crimes of witches were no longer to be considered by the courts. The net result of this turn of affairs was that victims of black magic more and more took matters into their own hands in an effort to gain redress and to halt the activities of notorious practitioners of sorcery. How many innocent people in isolated mountain villages suffered persecution and physical attack cannot be known, but two instances that came to public notice and received newspaper coverage indicate the seriousness of the problem.

The first case, reported in a Santa Fe journal, tells of an episode that nearly produced fatal results.

Persons just returned from Tierra Amarilla, where the Rio Arriba county court was in session last week, advise of a trial before Chief Justice Axtell, which recalls the dark deeds of centuries ago, when torture and even the stake were resorted to as persuasives in cases where confessions were wanted, renunciations of faith were desired, or withheld information was sought to be exhorted. This modern barbarity occurred in Tierra Amarilla in the year of our Lord, 1882. The offender is Felipe Madrid, and his victim was a woman with whom years ago he was intimate. Felipe had broken off relations with his sometime associate, and after years of promiscuous distribution of attention to other females was seized by a loathsome disease. After months of suffering he conceived that he had been bewitched by the woman alluded to, and whose name the writer could not learn. He was encouraged in this by Cipriano Medino, and other associates, and finally determined to free himself of the spell by adopting the only course known to the believers in witchcraft, which course is to make the offending witch cure the patient, and if she refuses, to whip her to death.

Accordingly he sent three men from Tierra Amarilla to Abiquiu with instructions to bring the woman to his house. They obeyed, and when they had brought her to him Madrid tied her up by the hands in his house, and told her if she did not cure him he would whip her to death. She protested her innocence and declared her inability to effect the cure, whereupon Madrid whipped her with a "black snake" until she was very nearly dead. She at last promised to cure him, being willing to promise anything in order to be released.

Madrid let her down intending to renew the whipping if she failed to make her promise good. The woman, to gain time, called for ointments and medicines and finally succeeded in escaping from the house, whence she made her way back to Abiquiu.

The matter was brought to the attention of the grand jury and an indictment for assault and battery was the result. The case being tried the prisoner was fined $150 and costs, that being the extent of the law in the case, as the prisoner was in a state of health which would not admit of his being imprisoned.[2]

Another Rio Grande paper several years later gave brief details of an even more unfortunate incident.

Major T. D. Burns, merchant of Tierra Amarilla brings in word of a shocking outrage that occurred recently in Rio Arriba County. A Mexican woman, aged about 40 years, whom the natives of the small village known as Chimayo believed to be a witch in league with the Devil, was taken from her lonely adobe hut by three roughs on Thursday last and murdered. They stripped her of all her clothing and shot and stabbed her many times. It is said the perpetrators of the crime are known to the authorities, but are desperate characters and no attempt whatever has been made to arrest them.[3]

Such newspaper accounts indicate that the subject of witchcraft, even if disdained in the eyes of the new Anglo-American law, was nonetheless surviving along the Rio Grande in the latter half of the nineteenth century. And since the end of that century a body of witch lore has in fact been made available in copious detail.

Practically every adobe hamlet and town on the Rio Grande once possessed its own stories and traditions of witches, were-animals, and supernatural events. Although the details might vary from one region to another, a basic pattern of witchcraft belief prevailed throughout the Southwest and northern Mexico, so that a certain uniformity is discernible in all activities related to the practice of occult arts. For example, from extreme southeast Texas to the mountains of southern Colorado, Hispano witches generally acknowledged three ways by which they attained their macabre powers. First, some persons at birth were fated to receive an evil endowment by which they were inexorably led into a career devoted to witchery. Since this power came unbidden, the witch had no choice but to fulfill her destiny, and parents looked with foreboding upon any of their offspring exhibiting strange or deviant behavior. One Mexican explained it in this way: "It is unfortunate for a family to have a witch. Perhaps all the other children will be good, but one will show that she knows dark magic even when she is a child. Yes, it is hard for a family to have a witch."[4]

A second category of witches, and by far the largest in number, was that composed of persons who voluntarily took up the craft, usually for the specific purpose of seeking revenge against their enemies. These were considered the most dangerous practitioners, because all their goals were bent toward doing harm to others. They magnified any small offense and repaid the slight many times over with an abominable curse. Their education and initiation was ordinarily handled by someone already adept in the ways of sorcery as in the case of a woman of the village of Las Placitas east of Albuquerque.

Juanita frequently visited the house of an avowed witch, Felicia. Because of her unbridled temper and selfishness, Juanita alienated many of her neighbors and even members of her own family, and to punish them she desired to learn the techniques of bewitchment. She begged Felicia to teach her all she knew, and the witch consented. She showed Juanita how to prepare herbs and make them work, and she helped her assemble a collection of little bags and stuff them with the hair of people and different animals. These bags were to be fastened inside her petticoat and worn at all times. To save her from the power of other witches, Felicia instructed her pupil in the manufacture and use of a magic doll, filling it with hair from every living thing they could find. Finally the witch presented her last lesson, demonstrating how Juanita might fly in the night on the wind by raising her arms and calling out, "I go without God and without the Holy Virgin."[5]

Occasionally advanced practitioners conducted formal schools for the imparting of esoteric knowledge to students. These graduates in witchcraft, called *arbularias*, held classes where beginners learned how to bewitch, cast spells, and transform themselves into a variety of objects and animals. Most of this instruction followed the classic methods of Old World sorcery with the addition of a few variations in the magical arts derived from the Indians. Legend maintains that a school for aspiring witches was long active at Peña Blanca in central New Mexico, where apprentices entered a cave and attended classes conducted by the Devil and graduate sorcerers. The beginner learned to transform himself into a dove, then into an owl, and finally into a dog.[6]

The final variety of witches was that made up of individuals who deliberately sold their souls to the Devil in exchange for power and wealth. In New Mexico they were spoken of as being in agreement with the Devil (*pactado con el Diablo*). The Satanic witches, unlike those in the two previous categories, did not operate alone, but banded together in groups to compound the force of their magic.[7] This kind of witch, too, was educated to the trade, but her goal was less that of reaping revenge against personal enemies, and more one of commercial gain. She dispensed her services for a fee, agreeing to bewitch a client's enemy for a fixed price.

Satan's witches customarily entered into a pact during a highly ritualized conclave held by the Devil's children. Assemblies or "Sabbats" figured prominently in European witch cults, and it is clear that this feature was originally carried intact from Spain by colonial immigrants to the Rio Grande. Those making a compact with the Devil and attending ceremonial gatherings seldom disclosed the nature of their clandestine activity, but descriptions of witch assemblies were given from time to time by persons who accidentally stumbled upon one or were lured to a meeting by a witch acquaintance hoping to win a convert.

Conclaves, whether for the initiation of new members or for the simple performance of periodic rites, as a rule included these features: unrestrained dancing, feasting, and merry-making; the presence of a goat — one of the traditional forms of the Devil — whose tail the revelers solemnly kissed; and the entrance of a giant snake that embraced each member of the throng. The celebrations commenced at sundown, lasted all night, and ended at dawn. According to most accounts they were carried out in dismal, remote places, such as a cave or deep arroyo, far from the prying eyes of the curious. However, in some villages known to be infested by witches, Devil-worshipers brazenly met in deserted buildings in the very heart of the community.

About the turn of the present century, a youth named Matias was riding horseback late at night and entered the town of Arroyo Seco. The only light appeared to come from a ruined building on the main plaza, and as he approached he could see through a broken window that people inside were dancing. Dismounting, he went to the front door, but the main hall suddenly became quiet and dark, and a strange feeling came over him. He rapidly climbed back on his horse and started away, but glancing over his shoulder, he observed the bright lights flickering on again and saw the wild dancing resume. These weird events left no doubt in his mind that he had chanced upon a party of witches.[8]

Another man, living south of Taos, was introduced to a

Devil's assembly in a more curious manner. He noticed that on certain nights a number of his aunts and uncles drove hurriedly from town in an old buggy. Mystified, he decided to conceal himself beneath the vehicle and accompany his relatives on their nocturnal journey. No sooner had he tied himself to the undercarriage than the group climbed aboard and drove away at breakneck speed. Soon they were in unfamiliar country that abounded in strange vegetation. Reaching their destination, the men and women descended and entered a house almost hidden by the steep walls of an arroyo. The man followed and crawled under a window through which he could see a room full of witches all frolicking about. Soon a door opened, and a huge billy goat walked in and made a circle around the witches who all kissed his tail. The goat left and was followed by an enormous snake that slithered across the floor and kissed each member of the crowd with his tongue. Finally four men dressed in black paraded across the room and laid down a coffin. From this they pulled out a corpse, and the elated witches, like a pack of hungry wolves, fell upon the body and began to eat it. The terrified eavesdropper ran back and hid himself again under the buggy, and presently his ghoulish relatives returned and drove home.[9]

Charles Lummis, while collecting witch stories along the upper Rio Grande in the 1880s, learned of a man named Patapalo who was something of the village idiot in San Mateo. One day a friend, José, approached him and said, "Patapalo, why are you so stupid? Come with me tonight and I will make you the wisest man in the world, so that you can play any music, speak any language, and even know what happens a hundred miles away." Any Hispano but a simpleton would have recognized at once that this was an open invitation to become a witch, but Patapalo innocently fell into the trap, and later he revealed to Lummis the particulars of his unnerving experience.

"That night about eight o'clock José came for me, and we started walking across the plain. After a half hour we found ten thousand mesquite bushes and on each one hung a rosary. I was often there before but never saw a single mesquite. I said, 'What is this thing?' but José replied, 'Keep your tongue to your teeth and come on.' At that moment we came to a great door with an iron lock, and a voice from within called, 'Who's there?' José said, 'We are two. One is ignorant.' Then the door opened, and we went into a room, so large I could not see the end of it. There was a bright light and I saw hundreds of people, the men on one side and the women on the other. Many of them I knew from Socorro and other places. In the middle were dozens of musicians with all classes of instruments and when they played very fine music, the men and women danced together.

"Such fine dancers I have never seen. Then a very large goat came in and spoke to all, and everybody had to kiss him. And when the goat had gone there was a snake — of larger body than mine — that came in upright. And it moved to every man and wound itself around him and put its tongue in his mouth, and the same to every woman. And when he did so, they talked words that I could not understand. But when he came to me and put his face before mine, my heart left me, and I cried, 'Jesus, Mary, Joseph, save me!' And at that instant I was standing alone in the plain. The snake, José, and the people were gone, and there remained only a strong smell of sulphur. I walked home a long way very much alarmed.

"Next day I saw José and he said, 'Fool! The snake was ready to give you the tongue of wisdom, but you called the holy name and ruined all.' He wanted me to go again, but I was afraid and never did."[10]

This same tale involving a visit to a witch assembly, the performance of a goat and snake, and the instantaneous disappearance of the scene upon uttering the names of the Holy Family, occurs with only little variation from the San Luís Valley in Colorado to El Paso on the middle Rio Grande. A slightly different version tells of a youth borne through the air to a witches' dance after he has been required to deposit his rosary and scapular on a tree. As he joins in the feast, he finds a human fingernail in one of the dishes and puts it in his pocket, intending to take it home and show his mother, whom he suspects of being a witch. The goat and snake enact their roles, and when the latter approaches him for the diabolical kiss, his courage fails, he acclaims the sacred names, and finds himself alone in the desert. After a three-day journey home, he tells his mother about the experience and shows her the fingernail. She scolds him for his cowardice and informs him that he lost a big opportunity, confirming his suspicion that she is a witch.[11]

In Europe, assemblies of witches or Sabbats by custom took place regularly four times a year: on February 2, the eve of May 1, on August 1, and on November-eve (All Hallow E'en). No such schedule seems to have survived among latter-day group sorcerers in the Southwest, although certain days of the week had special meaning. Here, as remains true in Mexico at present, Tuesdays and Fridays were regarded as witches' days, when any magic proved especially potent. Victims laboring under a spell often suffered pain or distress only on these days. Babies afflicted by bewitchment had to be cured before the following Friday or they invariably died.

For Hispano folk, Catholic Christianity offered the strongest bulwark and protection against the malicious arrows of witches, a stout shield behind which they could retreat and find security. As a safeguard against supernatural attack, the cross served as the most effective religious weapon. No mule drover setting out with a pack caravan would think of exposing his stock to needless danger from malign supernatural forces, so upon each long-eared animal's shoulder he carefully made a cross with cornmeal. Many persons raised an inconspicuous cross over their front doorway, believing its presence guaranteed that no witch could enter the house. Homeowners who neglected this precaution and discovered a witch in the family parlor protected themselves by making the sign of the cross.

The cross was also useful in identifying suspected witches,

since such persons have a natural fear of the symbol. A popular way was to place a cross made of two needles inside a broom and stand the broom behind the door. The witch would not be able to leave until it was removed or until a dog or another person passed through the doorway first.[12] A cross made of two broom straws and placed on the doorsill worked in a similar manner. The supposed witch would make several attempts to leave the room but would always turn back from the door with some excuse. Only when the charm had been removed could she depart. Many folk also believed that by placing a needle at the exit a witch had to go through the eye to escape the house.[13]

A Hispano girl from one of the Rio Grande towns once described a personal experience illustrating the efficacy of crosses in identifying a witch. "When I was a child," she related, "Doña Refugio, an old neighbor woman, lived by herself in an old adobe house down the road. People said she was a *bruja* ("witch"). I did not believe them.

" 'Very well. You shall see for yourself,' said my father. 'Witches are afraid of the cross. They will not go near it or over it under any circumstances. That *bruja*, Doña Refugio, is coming here this afternoon. Get me four needles. We will cross them and put them under the *saleas*.'

"At that time we used *saleas* before every door. They were sheepskin pelts that kept the cold wind from blowing under the door. I brought the needles. My father made a cross with two of them and placed it under the *salea* that leads into the kitchen.

"Doña Refugio came to see my mother that afternoon. While they were talking, with their backs turned to him, my father went to the *salea* beside the outside door where she had entered and placed two more needles in the form of a cross under the sheepskin. Then he went outside. In a few minutes he called in an excited voice, 'Doña Refugio! Doña Refugio! Come quickly. Your house is on fire.'

"Doña Refugio ran to the outside door. When she started to put her foot on the *salea*, she drew back as though it had burned her. She ran to the door going into the kitchen, but she would not step across that *salea* either. She ran around the room in circles, as though she was crazy, peering out the doors and windows but not daring to cross either *salea*.

" 'Take that *salea* away,' she cried to me. 'It's dirty. I cannot step on it.'

"My father came to the door and said, 'Never mind, Doña Refugio. Your house is all right. I went to see. It was only the smoke in the chimney.' Then fearing she would stay all afternoon, he kicked the *salea* away from the door.

" 'See, mamacita,' he said to my mother, 'you have lost two needles here under the *salea*.' As soon as the cross was out of the door, Doña Refugio ran to her house.

" 'Ah, ha!' said my father. 'Now we know you for the old *bruja* that you are.' "[14]

Another religious prophylactic serving to nullify the power of witchcraft was the pronouncement of holy phrases and formulas at moments of great danger. Exclaiming *Madre de Dios* ("Mother of God") or calling upon the name of God often was sufficient to break a spell at once. Reciting the words *Alavado sean los dulces nombres de Jesús, María, y José* ("Praise be the sweet names of Jesus, Mary, and Joseph") in front of a witch caused her temporary loss of power.[15] In a like manner, persons assailed by a witch frequently won a measure of protection by invoking the aid of saints. San Antonio, San Cirilio, and San Benito enjoyed the strongest reputations as capable patrons, affording some immunity for those threatened by evildoers. Wearing a San Benito medal helped keep witches at bay, probably because the saint's name derived from the Spanish word *bendito*, meaning "blessed."

Among Mexican-Americans of rural south Texas, a man rendered impotent by witchcraft could be cured in the following way: "Go to the nearest church, take from the lamp hanging in front of the Blessed Sacrament a few drops of oil, and with a clean rag anoint the genitalia. Drop a little more of the oil upon a pan of live coals, saying, 'I do this in the name of the Father, Son, and Holy Ghost.' Then seek the woman who is beloved, and all obstacles will disappear. But the witch who has caused all the trouble will soon die."[16]

All these devices associated with religion, had they been unfailingly effective, would, of course, have considerably reduced the terrors associated with bewitchment. However, the Devil, supported by his armies of witches and sorcerers, possessed a storehouse of tricks and hexes and from long experience knew cunning ways to evade the barriers imposed by Christianity. One tactic was to assault persons of weak faith or those dissipated by sin because they were unable to flee to the security of religion. Most Hispanos believed that devout churchmen remained impervious to enchantment, while backsliders ran a constant risk of falling victim to a spell.

One of the most curious aspects of witch lore along the Rio Grande was the conviction that men named Juan received special power to catch witches. A prominent New Mexican, Amado Chaves, described the accepted procedure in a letter to historian Charles Lummis in 1897. "Have I ever told you how we used to catch witches in New Mexico when I was young?" he wrote. "We would mark a large circle on the ground, as big as a room, and in the center set a man by the name of Juan with his shirt inside out. We did this on a dark night and invariably any witch who was near got into the circle and was caught. Sometime she would be in the shape of a fox, coyote, or black cat, but once inside the circle she became an old woman again. There are many interesting stories about this among our old people. You know one of the women thus caught. Do you remember Señora Chonita who used to work for Mr. Baca and lives near Rinconada? She is the one."[17]

In some accounts Juan's circle is mentioned as being precisely nine feet in circumference. Also, his capture of witches is facilitated if he shouts, "In the name of God I call thee *bruja*," or alternately *"Venga bruja!"* ("Come witch!").[18] Because so many persons were christened Juan, we might easily suppose that with a little labor on the part of each one, they quickly could have caught and exterminated all the witches in the Southwest. The fact was that although the Juans held this useful power, the majority feared to use it, knowing that other witches in the neighborhood might band together and whip them as punishment.

In another version of this theme, a boy named Juan may thwart a witch who enters a home in the form of some animal or bird. When this occurs, he turns his clothes inside out and draws a circle near the doorway. The witch then disappears, and on the following day may be found in her normal human form, but dead.[19]

The village of El Llano above Ranchos de Taos used to be a favored rendezvous for witches who would gather there, traveling as sparks of fire. One night two Juans decided to do a little hunting — of the kind for which they were famous. Going to El Llano, they stood opposite each other holding sticks, and as a spark dropped they marked a circle around it on the ground. Presently the sparks glimmered out and in their places sat women begging the two Juans to let them go. But the men continued drawing circles until they had ensnared a dozen or more howling witches. When they had identified each one, they released them.[20]

Juan Chavez, who lived in Tomé during the 1890s, gained considerable reputation for his ability to expose practitioners of the black craft. In his community lived an old woman, Chata, suspected of being a witch. On a summer day Juan left Tomé on horseback to visit a friend in Casa Colorado who had promised to give him a milk cow. As he was riding down an isolated stretch of road, he perceived a large ball of fire leaping over the countryside in great bounds. Recognizing that the ball was a transformed witch, he got down and drew a circle in the midst of the road. The flaming object then flew into the circle and vanished. Juan remounted his horse, continued the journey, and returned the next day by the same route leading his new cow. Arriving at the place where he had seen the fireball, he found the witch Chata sitting in the road inside his circle. They exchanged some pleasantries, and Juan invited the old woman to get up and accompany him to Tomé, since it was far too hot to be resting in the sun. Somewhat peevishly, the witch told him that she was unable to leave unless Juan gave her his hand. After he did this, she trailed him into Tomé in a manner very much subdued.[21]

The residents of La Madera in the northern foothills of the Sandía Mountains once experienced a period of harassment by witches. In the 1930s several elderly people told what they had done about this trouble. "When a witch cast an evil spell upon any of us, we set a Juan to catch her. He would go out into the night and watch for her. By and by, he would see the witch because she could never sense the presence of a Juan. When he saw her coming, he jerked off his shirt, turned it wrong side out and flung it in her path. There was no way a witch could see this shirt, and she got tangled in it, sprawled on the ground, and was unable to move. Early in the morning, the townspeople would come and take her to the houses of persons she had hexed. They made her cure them and threatened her with death if she worked her magic again. Then everyone seized switches and lashed the witch out of the village."[22]

A distinct idea that surfaces wherever witchcraft is practiced is the belief that black magic may be turned against the person originally dispensing it. If this can be done, the victim recovers and his fate is delivered back to the spellbinder. A witch in Las Placitas gave a neighbor a bowl of doctored hominy for his dinner to even an old score. The recipient suspected treachery, added a few ingredients to the bowl to disguise it, and sent it back as his gift. The witch innocently ate her own concoction, and for the next three years withered away by degrees, finally succumbing on the feast of San Antonio in 1939.[23]

Another case in which a witch's evil boomeranged is reported from the village of Cieneguilla a few miles below Santa Fe. Doña Vicenta Lopez became ill and none of the local herbalists succeeded in diagnosing her complaint. At first a small red spot appeared on one cheek, but this soon spread and the whole face appeared to be rotting away. In alarm her husband hitched up his wagon and team and drove her to the doctors in Santa Fe. They too were mystified and sent the poor woman home to die.

Shortly afterward a crippled Indian stopped at the Lopez door and asked for overnight lodging. The husband replied that there was no room since his children had all returned home to be with their failing mother. The Indian expressed sympathy and offered to try to work a cure. After he had seen Doña Vicenta, he said, "Let me stay three days, for in that time I can heal her. But you must watch the house, *patrón*, for someone will come in these days who has put this sickness upon her."

Señor Lopez remained vigilant and on the third day a neighbor woman came toward the house. But she paused at the gate and turned back. The same evening his wife began to get well and in gratitude he heaped presents upon the Indian. Later he learned that the neighbor who had turned at the gate had come down with the same illness, and three days later she was dead. The Indian had known that a witch would come, and he had managed to turn the evil spell back upon her.

As is apparent from some of the episodes already related, witches caught in the plying of their evil craft might be subjected to beatings or even suffer summary execution. Flogging was a stock punishment for a variety of crimes during colonial days and its use continued among backward rural folk long after Anglo-American occupation. The whip not only chastised wrongdoers, but in the case of witches, its liberal application might force revocation of a spell or lifting of a curse. An unequivocal threat of execution could produce the same end.

The wife of Juan Baca once refused coffee to a witch named Salia, who went away angry. The next day a sore formed on Señora Baca's nose and small, white pebbles commenced to drop from the nostrils. Juan knew exactly what was the matter, and going to Salia's house he told her, "Look, you have bewitched my wife. If you don't cure her immediately, I'm going to hang you."

The witch proved quite amenable under the shadow of a noose and consented to effect a remedy, so Juan returned home content. But his Señora grew worse instead of improving and he was consumed by anger. Taking a braided reata he went again to Salia's and announced, "I have come to hang you."

"No, no, don't," the witch cried. "I'll come right over." And she accompanied him back to his house. There she gave the sick woman a little black powder and rubbed her nose. Out came a sinew four inches long and the offending nose was healed.[24]

This incident occurred in the community of San Mateo in the mid-1880s, when the town's residents were enduring a siege of trouble promoted by a local coven of witches. Another reputed member of this devilish sorority was Marcelina, a desiccated and poverty-stricken little woman in her fifties. Somehow Don José Patricio Mariño, according to his own claim, incurred Marcelina's displeasure, and she turned him into a woman. He passed several months in this unnatural state until he succeeded in arranging with another witch in the distant canyon of Juan Tafoya to restore his manhood. Marcelina bewitched several other San Mateo residents, including a Señor Motano whom she caused to go lame. Finally in 1887, her neighbors rose in indignation and stoned her to death.[25]

Nearby in the smaller village of San Rafael lived three celebrated witches to whose careers a veritable litany of outrages were linked. Charles Lummis held, in his words, "the unprecedented privilege of photographing these women as they stood in the door of their little adobe house — Antonia Morales and Placida Morales, sisters, and Villa, the daughter of Placida, and not more than seventeen years old." (See Plate 1.) Like Marcelina in San Mateo, the Morales witches once transformed a young man into a female. Handsome

Francisco Ansures unsuspectingly drank a cup of their coffee and a few minutes later was horrified to see that his hair had grown two feet in length, his coarse overalls had turned to petticoats, and a pleasant tenor voice had become a squeaky treble. He was no more dismayed than his wife, and the pair scraped together enough money to pay another witch to raise the curse. The Morales sisters escaped punishment for this baleful deed, only because the people of San Rafael held them in such awe and dread.[26]

Stories of this nature were common fare among the Hispano population of the Southwest. Steeped in supernatural beliefs, the simple folk had no doubts as to the reality and potency of black magic and witchcraft. This implicit faith was the source of much misery and distress, as we have seen, and both the accused witch and her supposed victim, swept to their fate by popular delusion, needlessly suffered the consequences of man's folly.

PLATE 1. *Three witches of San Rafael, 1885.* Left to right: *Villa Morales, age 17; Placida Morales, her mother; and Antonia Morales, her aunt. (Charles Lummis photograph)*

4

The Ways of Witches

IN THE LONG HISTORY of witchcraft in the Western World, magicians and sorcerers have become associated in the popular mind with certain standard techniques and procedures used in the carrying out of their peculiar functions. Signing a compact in blood with the Devil and renouncing Christianity, forming cults and engaging in obscene revelry, foretelling future events, and the laying of spells and incantations upon innocent victims constitute some of the more conventional activities of witches. Contributing further to a stereotype are the common adjuncts of the black cat, flying broom, pointed hat, and steaming caldron of mysterious brew. Examination of the records shows that most such notions and action patterns crystallized and became integrated into a new system of supernatural belief during the Middle Ages, but that the elements themselves had their origin in the pagan religions of antiquity.

Hispano or Mexican witches of the Southwest, as heirs of this ancient legacy, made use of the familiar methods of sorcery and in numerous particulars conformed to the style of occultism developed by their European forebears. Yet because of their isolation and the influence of Indian magical-religious practices, the tools and techniques of their witchery emerged with a distinctive stamp. A survey of these within the province of the Rio Grande unveils a fascinating web of folk belief unlike that found anywhere else and lays open a little-known chapter in the history of supernaturalism.

In those not so remote days when witchcraft was a subject of almost universal concern, the average person went about his daily affairs warily, for he never knew at what moment he might unwittingly incur the wrath of one of Satan's lackeys. He stepped cautiously around cats with glowing eyes, shunned hooting owls, avoided food offered him by any unusual hands, gazed with trepidation upon all shadowy, night-flying objects, and kept a sharp lookout for werewolves and other such animals. When illness or misfortune struck him down unexpectedly and defied explanation by ordinary means, he anxiously searched his back trail to see if some chance occurrence or unlooked-for encounter with a witch might have precipitated supernatural retribution. His legions of fears were inculcated at an early age when around the winter hearth grandparents spun tales of horror and poured forth the hellish deeds of sorcerers, the grim details remaining indelibly impressed on his mind until death.

As every simple child and adult knew without question, witches possessed the power to soar at will, high and with uncanny speed, above the moonlit Rio Grande, over the loftiest mountain ranges, and across the cactus flats and deserts from south Texas to Arizona. As in the Old World and elsewhere, in America the broom was a common instrument of locomotion, but other conveyances such as gourds, pumpkins, eggs, and especially fireballs furnished means of travel. The witch anointed with magic ointment whatever she had chosen to ride, ascended her chimney, and sailed across the night sky. This adhered closely to flying methods known in Europe where sorceresses oiled themselves and their magic sticks with pomade, murmured incantations, and raced through the air to a Devil's sabbat.

Most witches launched their flight with the words *Sin Dios y sin Santa María* ("Without God and without the Virgin Mary"). If by chance the formula was pronounced incorrectly, they remained suspended in the air, unable to fly. Once several young girls in Santa Fe spent the night with an old woman. In the hour after midnight, they saw her rise, rub her body with ointment, repeat the formula, and fly away. Thinking it would be fun to follow suit, they emulated the procedure, but upon being lifted up, they became frightened, exclaimed "Jesus, Mary, and Joseph," and fell to the ground.[1] Some people claimed to have been carried on a witch's back thousands of miles a minute to a distant location, but when they became alarmed and cried "God save me!" they instantly fell hundreds of feet and landed without harm. Others reported that when they attempted to fly like witches, they neglected some aspect of the prescribed ritual and crashed into the ceiling.

On night excursions, witches generally retained their human form, but sometimes, to facilitate their goings, they assumed the legs and eyes of a coyote or other animal, leaving their own at home. One night Juan Perea, a notorious male witch who died in San Mateo in 1888, sallied forth on a nocturnal ramble after depositing his eyes in a saucer on the kitchen table and borrowing those of a cat. While he was away, his hungry dog upset the table and gobbled up his eyes, leaving Juan to spend the rest of his life wearing the green eyes of the cat.[2]

Lorenzo Labadie of Las Vegas, New Mexico, a man of prominence and one not readily succumbing to superstition, unknowingly hired a witch in the 1890s as nurse for his baby. Several months later a ball was given at Puerta de Luna, one hundred miles south, and friends of his were astonished to see the nurse and baby there. When asked the whereabouts of Señor Labadie and his family, the nurse replied that they were visiting at a ranch a few miles distant but were too fatigued to attend the dance. On the following day, the friends went to the ranch and learned the Labadies had not been present at all. Suspecting the nurse to be a witch, they wrote a warning to Don Lorenzo, who knew only that his infant and its keeper were in his house when he went to bed, and there also when he woke up. Since it was plain the nurse was a witch who indulged in night-flying, he promptly discharged her.[3]

Sometimes for a fee or even out of a perverse sense of charity, witches assisted other people to make long voyages by air. Rosalia, a woman of Arroyo Hondo, had not received news from her son, who was herding sheep on the plains of Wyoming, and she consulted a local witch named Honsha.

"I will take you to visit your son, if you let me blindfold you first," Honsha said.

Rosalia agreed and permitted her eyes to be covered with a red handkerchief. As she smelled the pungent odor of burning herbs, she felt herself lifted into space and shortly she landed in a high tree. Below she saw her son eating lunch by a camp fire, but as she started to speak to him, he vanished and she found herself again in her own house. A week later when he returned, the son related that one day while eating his lunch a strange feeling possessed him. An owl alighted on the tree above him, but as he raised his gun to shoot, it disappeared. From that moment forward, he felt a great longing to return home. The date and hour of the owl apparition corresponded exactly with the day the witch had flown Rosalia to see her son.[4]

As we have seen, witches may roam the skies as balls of fire. It is practically impossible to convince a person who has seen an enchanted and flaming sphere that the spectacle was nothing more than a comet or meteor, for he is familiar with the chronicles of Rio Grande witch lore detailing the host of flights undertaken in this manner. Self-professed authorities declare they have observed luminescent balls jumping about through the pine forests and around the houses of witches, performing a ritualistic dance in their mad hopping.[5] Nicolás Mariño of San Mateo beheld a fireball descending into an arroyo and going to investigate discovered that it had turned into a huge rat. As he chased it through the tall grass, it suddenly changed into a dog, gave a savage growl, sprang over his head and disappeared among the willows. His fearless pursuit was not typical of most people who spied a devilish fireball.[6]

Two men were traveling the road to Chama late one December night when about one o'clock they caught sight of phantasmal light in the distance. At first they concluded it must be a campfire of wood-gatherers, but drawing closer they saw it change shape and make unearthly motions. Finally the light soared upward and shot across the horizon to the town of San Luís. The men went to a nearby house to inquire about the strange phenomenon, and there found a farmer suffering from bewitchment. What they had seen, he informed them, was his tormentor who returned nightly as a fireball.[7]

Closely connected with the aspect of flying was animal metamorphosis, or the transformation of witches into were-beasts. In Mexico it is necessary to make offerings of incense to pagan deities and request their permission to fly through the air in animal form, but north of the Rio Grande other methods were used.[8] Here initiates in the craft of witchery may take the form of wolves, cats, birds, or whatever creature they wish by an exercise of their own evil will and the muttering of an appropriate incantation. Assumption of an animal shape allows greater freedom of movement, but if goodly people recognize them in this disguise, they may be chased and killed. A wound inflicted on a witch while it is masquerading as a were-animal is believed to be visible when the individual resumes human form.

Manuel Lujan, a sheepherder, was sent by his *patrón* to deliver a flock of sheep in Valencia County. After a hard day's drive he encamped at the Valverde ford on the Rio Grande, cooked his supper, and lay down to sleep. During the night, he awoke and saw a coyote eating a piece of beef carelessly left by the fire. Taking his rifle, he fired and wounded it, but the animal escaped in the darkness. Early in the morning he struck the trail north with his flock and soon came upon some faint human footprints. Manuel felt a twinge of surprise because he knew that no people lived in that stretch of country, except Navajos who always traveled on horseback. Following the tracks to see if they belonged to someone lost or needing help, he shortly stumbled upon a puddle of blood. Fearing there might have been an Indian massacre close by, he hurried on until he reached a cottonwood grove where he found an old woman bleeding profusely from a wound in her shoulder. While he bound up the hurt, he asked her if she had been shot by the Indians.

The old crone glared at him fiercely and shouted, "No! You shot me."

Astonished, Manuel denied shooting at anyone on his trip. But the woman put him straight when she announced that her wound had been received at his campfire the previous night. The poor sheepherder paled visibly with the realization that he was dealing with a witch. Afraid that she might take revenge by bestowing a curse upon him, he offered to conduct her to the nearest town for medical aid. With some haste he deposited her at a small hospital in Los Lunas and continued on his journey, glad to escape the coyote-witch and a near brush with supernatural disaster.[9]

A party of Pueblo Indians were once riding horseback when they chanced upon a magnificent black mare. Knowing that no one thereabouts owned such an animal, they gave chase and followed it into a willow thicket. But instead of a horse, the riders found a panting and perspiring old witch who claimed that nothing had passed that way. The Indians held a swift conference, reasoned that the mare had changed into the woman, and for safety decided they had better kill her. But when the witch begged for mercy for the sake of her children, they relented and spared her life on condition that she not become a mare again.[10]

Cats and owls are two ancient and universally feared heralds of witchcraft. A black cat is not only a companion and accomplice of witches, it occasionally serves as an ingredient in venomous potions. It also possesses an "invisible bone" that may be used as a charm and as a symbol that the owner is pledged to the Devil. This curious relic is obtained by casting a black cat without any blemishes into a pot of boiling water where it is stewed until the flesh falls from the bones. Then the bones are removed from the water and held one at a time in front of a mirror. The bone not visible is the charm.[11]

In numerous Southwestern tales, cats are associated with the loss of a witch's eyes. In some instances, the animal eats the eyes that have been removed and left behind when the enchantress goes night-voyaging. In others the witch loses her sight and is obliged to take and use the eyeballs of her pet.

Don Pánfilo, who died sometime during the early 1930s, was a lonely widower the last years of his life. He was often in the habit of passing a pleasant evening with two elderly sisters, his neighbors, playing a card game called Cañoncito. People warned him that the pair were *brujas* and would bewitch him, but he scoffed at the idea and declared that he was not afraid. The sisters bore a remarkable resemblance, the only noticeable difference being that the elder had eyes of a dark coffee color while the younger's were tea color flecked with gold.

Mysteriously the two would disappear each night and regularly on the following morning would reappear with dark circles under their eyes. Often when Don Pánfilo was winning at Cañoncito, he tried to persuade them to continue the game, but at a certain hour of the evening they always quit playing and told him to go home. When anyone asked him what his companions did after dark, he replied jokingly, "Well, maybe they go flying."

Although Don Pánfilo made a conspicuous show of not caring what the sisters did with their time, he was secretly filled with a great curiosity. Repeatedly he watched their house in the silent hours of the night, but no one ever left or returned, and the only unusual signs were two lean cats with glittering eyes that hissed and arched their backs whenever he approached. In the late afternoon while playing Cañoncito, the women would speak of things that had happened the night before in the neighborhood, and Pánfilo would discover these things were true.

Finally, in exasperation he resolved to clear away the doubts in his mind, and, walking to the sisters' house at midnight, he knocked at the door. For once the cats were nowhere about, and as he waited for someone to answer, he prepared an excuse to explain his calling at this unusual hour. But when he rapped again and the house remained still, Don Pánfilo pushed at the door and found it open. Inside, the rooms were empty, a few small flames flickered in the corner fireplace, and something eerie glistened on the hearth. Drawing closer he perceived with a thump of horror two pairs of human eyes reposing on the warm stones. One set was coffee-colored and the other of lighter hue with green and gold flecks.

As the eyes stared at him, the poor man was almost overcome by a profound feeling of sickness. Taking a heavy iron spoon from the kitchen table, he scooped up the glaring orbs and dumped them in the fire. Instantly they began to pop and sputter over the coals and dance high up the chimney. Thoroughly frightened now, Pánfilo tried to recover the eyes with his spoon, but it was too late. They had burned and shriveled until they looked like hard black walnuts. At that moment the two lean cats dashed into the room and ran about mewing and wailing. The intruder made a hasty sign of the cross and fled.

The next day Don Pánfilo found himself in a quandary. He was afraid to go to the sisters' house as usual, yet he feared they would suspect him if he did not. In the end, screwing up his courage, he went to their door, affecting a jolly and innocent manner.

"*Pase! Pase*, Don Pánfilo," one of the women called, and he went in. The sisters spoke to him cordially, but kept their faces turned away. They both stumbled over chairs and tables as though they could scarcely see. Then they informed him in sad voices that they were so busy the card game would have to be permanently suspended.

Looking more closely, the visitor saw that each of the sisters was wearing the round eyes of a cat and that they moved about as if the daylight bothered them. When the two cats crept from under a bed, he noticed they were blind, for there were no eyes in their sockets. With as much discretion as he could muster, Pánfilo made a quick retreat. Thereafter, when anyone inquired about his strange friends, he always shrugged off the questions, saying, "Who knows what they do at night, or where they go? As for me, I no longer leave my house after dark. And I lock my doors and windows."[12]

As much or more so than black cats, owls were regarded as omens of ill-luck and allies of witches. If a family heard hooting above its rooftop at night, it was a sure sign some evil was about to visit the home. If someone was sufficiently brave, he went outside and called to the owl, *"Mañana vendrás por sal."* ("Tomorrow you come for salt.") And the first person who visited the house on the following morning to make a request was identified as a witch.[13] Two owls heard chattering and talking posed a clear warning that disaster lurked near, and Hispanos avoided traveling or any other unusual activity until the danger had passed.[14]

A fruit merchant named Félix once made a profitable business trip and while returning home had an unusual experience involving owls, an experience he was later bold enough to relate at his own peril.

"It was growing late on the road and as I carried a lot of money, I didn't want to lay out overnight where I might be attacked and robbed. Presently the light from a house came into view, and approaching I called and asked if there was any lodging for a traveler. Two women responded, inviting me to stay the night, and fed me supper. I couldn't help feeling a phantasmal quality about the place and I noticed a strange cupboard in the corner filled with small boxes. One of the ladies led me into an adjacent room and showed me my bed. Since I was uneasy, I took my pistol and placed it under my pillow before going to sleep.

"Later I awoke and through the door, which was slightly ajar, I could see the women drying the dishes. When finished, they went and sat by the fireplace to smoke cornhusk cigarettes. One finally said to the other that I must be asleep now, and this frightened me because I thought they perhaps intended to kill me for my money. As they padded noiselessly into the room, my hand slipped up to the pistol, but they ignored me and proceeded to a dark corner of the chamber. Pulling out a shapeless bundle they spread its contents on the floor and one returned to the other room to get a couple of small boxes from the cupboard. Then I saw a strange and disconcerting thing. Both women removed their clothes, dusted their bodies with a mixture of powder from the boxes, took three steps in one direction and three in another, and hopped into a tub of water. Abruptly they changed into owls and emerged from the tub to fly about the gloomy house and eventually sail up the chimney.

"By now I was thoroughly dismayed, but being an inquisitive sort I got up and examined the small boxes. On the outside of each one I read, 'Magic Powder, San Antonio, Texas.' Feeling certain that when I told the story later people were going to ask me all sorts of questions, it seemed a good idea to learn as much as possible about this ghostly affair. For that reason I decided to go through the witches' ritual myself and see what happened.

"I threw off my clothes, covered my body with the two powders, took the necessary steps forward and backward, and leaped into the tub. But when I climbed out wet, I was still Félix. Nothing had happened. As I was drying myself on a blanket, I realized a medal of the Holy Child and a scapular of Our Lady of Carmel were still hanging around my neck and they might have prevented the magic from working. Removing these articles, I went through the whole formula again, and this time with an overwhelming suddenness I was transformed into an owl. Ascending the chimney, I perched on the roof and saw my horses grazing peacefully below in the moonlight. Then lifting my new wings, I rose above the piñon tops and joined a flock of owls. We eventually reached the site of a party at which all the guests were witches in the form of cats or owls. After a time I got scared they would recognize me as an interloper so I returned to the house. Again rubbing the powder, taking the steps, and dousing in the tub, I regained my human body and went back to bed.

"In the morning I got up and found the women at the breakfast table. Imagine my surprise when they asked me how I enjoyed the party. One of them advised me never to speak of the incident or some curse would surely befall me. But I like to talk and tell tales, and although I have since described this episode many times, I've so far escaped without suffering any harm. This may be because I refused the breakfast those two old witches offered me, for they could very easily have slipped something in my meal laying on me an infernal spell."[15]

A basic tenet of Hispano witch-faith holds that an offering of food or drink from persons of evil intent may be contaminated and the source of a supernatural malady or scourge. It is best to lay aside any product known to have come from a witch's kitchen for a period of three days, for within that time if the food turns to worms, its accursed nature is verified. Most simple folk simply threw away any gift that was suspect, being careful to hide their act from the donor. As the provident used to say, *"Brujas* mix dishes with strange and dangerous herbs. Who can foretell the evil effects of such food?"[16]

Those unwittingly or recklessly consuming what a witch proffers often find to their sorrow that some animal, alive and gnawing, forms in their stomach. A similar article of faith still prevails among many Indian people of Mexico who believe that when a conjurer looks inside their bellies for a source of illness he finds frogs, snakes, toads, worms, rats, lizards, dogs, and even hard-shelled armadillos.[17] Mexican-Americans on the lower Rio Grande know that witches bring sickness by sending "Satanic works" into the body of a victim. Between jobs the little creatures are stored in a bottle of milk.[18]

A woman in northern New Mexico was given a large cheese by a neighbor whom she suspected of dealing in black magic. When she cut the cheese at the table, she quietly slipped the first slice into her apron pocket because she had heard that an evil spell was always in this piece. Later, when no one was looking, she threw the cheese wedge to her dog. A few days later the dog grew thin and sick, and her sons, upon investigating, found it swarming with worms.[19]

The town drunk in Cebolleta some years ago went on a spree and injudiciously kicked and pummeled a witch. In revenge she caused a live mouse to grow in his stomach. After sobering up, he found himself in a state of perfect misery as the little rodent frolicked about under his belt. Contritely and with a substantial bribe in hand, he sought out the witch and persuaded her to coax the irksome mouse out through his mouth.[20]

In addition to causing harm through enchanted food or by introducing animals into a person's body, witches of the far Southwest knew the secrets of image magic. This form of wonder-working is quite ancient, for we know that the early Egyptians employed wax dolls and other figurines in their conjuring practices. Witches in south Texas even today hex their victim by sticking pins in a doll or by burying his photograph while reciting an incantation.[21]

In the mountain villages of southern Colorado and New Mexico, a witch's stock of charms and amulets inevitably included a collection of bewitched dolls. Pierced with cactus thorns, they brought excruciating pain and ultimately death upon intended victims. The only remedy was to buy off the witch, or failing in that, to threaten her with bodily harm if the spell was not lifted.

A Hispano lad living in one of the Rio Grande villages once quarreled with two Pueblo Indian boys. Later he became violently ill and the father discovered the Indians had threatened to bewitch him. He went to the boys' home and, after giving them a sound beating, obtained their promise to cure his son. Taking out a mud figure, the pair extracted several cactus needles and then destroyed the image. When the man returned home, he found his son had recovered.[22]

Still another mode of injurious magic, and one of equal antiquity, was the *mal ojo*, or "evil eye." The condition resulting from its application is actually a folk disease, producing symptoms of fever, crying, diarrhea, loss of weight, and usually leading to death. Children are more commonly afflicted and parents try to protect them by avoiding persons who stare intensely or show any peculiar quality in their eyes. Witches deliberately spread evil eye sickness, while some persons, born with excessively strong vision, do so unintentionally. Hispanos explain that *mal ojo* works because a forceful individual may knowingly or unwittingly captivate someone weaker, especially a woman or child, through a powerful glance which drains the victim of his will to act and saps his healthful energies. Mexican-Americans of the lower Rio Grande Valley of Texas generally ascribe a case of serious illness to an accidental encounter with the evil eye, while Spanish-speaking people of New Mexico and Colorado as a rule see a premeditated attack by a witch as the cause.[23] In instances of the former, the best recourse is to identify the person responsible and request him to pat the patient's head or rub his temples, producing an instantaneous cure. Such persons willingly comply and take no offense since they are aware of the strength of their eyesight and regret any harm it causes others.[24] But if a witch is the guilty party, a remedy may be difficult or impossible to obtain.

In addition to shielding their infants from the gaze of suspicious strangers, parents took other measures to ward off the evil eye. If the baby had been displayed in a crowd, as at Sunday Mass, where many people might have viewed and admired it, the mother afterward touched its forehead and whispered *"Dios te guarde tan linda"* ("God keep you pretty baby"), believing these words helped break up any spell emanating from the *mal ojo*. Parents also placed a string containing a piece of jet or a coral bead around the necks of small children to counteract the evil eye.[25] The use of jet probably traces back to Medieval Spain where peasants of the northern provinces used amulets of hard coal for the same purpose.[26]

Several reported instances of *mal ojo* from the Southwest will indicate something of its nature and practice and illustrate its place among folk superstitions of the area. Pepe, a resident of La Madera, New Mexico, had a slight cast in his left eye. If he chanced to enter a room and look at a newborn baby, for a certainty that baby would die. If he ventured into a kitchen and gazed at a cake about to be set in the fireplace to bake, nothing could prevent the cake from falling and being unfit to eat. For these reasons, Pepe was an object of fear and his neighbors evaded him as discreetly as possible.[27]

Two young boys of the village of Manzano east of Albuquerque attended a local fiesta in honor of *Nuestra Señora de Dolores*. Several Indians from Isleta Pueblo were there selling fruit, and they looked upon the lads in a malevolent way. Later they both developed a sickness diagnosed as a case of the evil eye, and in spite of the efforts to save them, they died.[28]

A young father in south Texas once took his family across the Rio Grande to visit relatives in Old Mexico. When he got home, he discovered that his tiny daughter was suffering from a high temperature, and thinking back, he remembered that a Mexican woman had looked endearingly at the child and had reached out to caress it. After several days the girl remained feverish, so he recrossed the river, located the presumed agent of *mal ojo*, urged her to touch the child, and when she did, the trouble subsided.[29]

In the practice of southwestern witchcraft, the *piedra iman*, or "ordinary lodestone," figures prominently. The ancient Romans believed the stone magnet possessed power and a life of its own and should be fed with iron filings. Their notions were carried throughout Europe and eventually reached Mexico and the Rio Grande frontier. Hispano witches acquiring a lodestone expanded their supernatural powers enormously as it gave them superior knowledge and eased their transformation into any animal or desired shape. To maintain its potency, they fed it needles, steel particles, and water every Friday. If this duty was neglected the owner pined away and died, or if the stone was misplaced or stolen, he lost his mind and dried up into a skeleton.[30] Many people kept a *piedra iman* around the house as protection against witchcraft and as a good luck piece or love amulet.

Although some of the principal techniques and paraphernalia used by witches in performance of their activities have been described in this chapter, it must be admitted that the actual mechanics for laying a hex or casting a spell are seldom clear. This is the case because witches contrive their magic in secret and exclude witnesses from their workshops. Their occult formulas and modes of operation are jealously guarded and only shared with another witch, who may be asked to pay for this privileged knowledge. Such information as is usually available comes mainly from witchcraft victims, their families and friends, persons scarcely qualifying as impartial observers. However, until the diary or memoirs of a witch come to light, we shall have to depend upon these secondhand sources for enlightenment regarding supernatural practices along the Rio Grande.

5

Pueblo Witchcraft

BELIEF IN WITCHCRAFT and in manipulation of supernatural powers for evil purposes was practically universal among American Indians. Many of the rites and customs of black magic indulged in by inhabitants of the New World bore striking resemblance to practices found in Europe, Africa, the South Seas, and elsewhere, for in whatever tribe or environment the craft appeared, there could be found the common belief that blame for human suffering often rested upon deliberate misuse of otherworldly powers by persons versed in the black arts.

Many Indian modes of bewitching paralleled those reported in Europe and New England. Native witches sought locks of hair, nail parings, saliva, urine, or fragments of perspiration-stained clothing from their prey so that these might be employed in occult treatments to produce disease or misfortune. Among tribes of the Northwest Coast, witches made images of enemies, then tortured those parts of the body in which they desired to instill pain. The Chippewa of the Great Lakes followed similar practice, except their images were not dolls or effigies, but figures drawn in the sand or the ashes of a campfire.[1] Among the ancient Aztecs of Mexico, doll-like representations of *amatl* paper were fashioned to serve the needs of witches.[2] The Tarahumara of the Sierra Madre of Chihuahua dispensed with images and relied upon a rasping stick and song to cause injury or death, to adversely control the weather, or to provoke other misfortune.[3]

A technique for bewitching encountered among most Indian groups involved the injection of some foreign object into a victim, such as an arrowhead, spearpoint, or piece of bone. Witches accomplished this, not through direct physical means, but by symbolic propulsion or by exerting mental energy. The Haida believed witches introduced mice inside a person's body and that if these could be expelled health returned.[4] The Cheyenne of the Great Plains used the "intrusion theory" to explain serious illness, and their medicine men, employing supernatural rites, were called upon to locate and extract the disturbing element.[5] Most tribes attributed to an evil medicine man the power to draw out a person's soul and fill the vacuum with the spirit of an animal or snake.

For native peoples of the New World no crime loomed more heinous nor brought swifter retribution than that of witchcraft. Often, mere suspicion resulted in condemnation and execution. Had a victim many relatives or friends, further bloodshed might follow if they sought revenge. Yet more frequently, execution of a witch served a useful therapeutic function for the society as a whole: with removal of the scapegoat upon whom all blame had been heaped for things gone wrong, anxieties were relieved and the community or tribe felt purged of evil.

For the Pueblo Indians of the Southwest, the nature and extent of witchcraft belief is fairly well known since these people have been studied meticulously by anthropologists for almost eighty years. Moreover, as we have seen, Spanish-colonial records beginning in the seventeenth century contain many references to witches and their activities. These documents, including trial records, reports of the missionaries, and statements by civil officials, clearly reveal the long and intense involvement of the Pueblos with witchcraft and allied matters of an occult character.

Evidently the Pueblo Indians' concern with magical systems extends well back into prehistoric times, but of this, precise details are lacking since information supplied by

PLATE 2. *A Pueblo Indian witch, 1890. (George Wharton James photograph)*

archeology is generally restricted to aspects of material culture. Nevertheless, rock art (incised or painted pictures left on cliff faces or cave walls), fetishes, and other ceremonial objects that have been discovered and studied by scholars strongly suggest that witchcraft was a tangible and threatening reality to the earliest inhabitants of the Rio Grande Valley. Furthermore, Pueblo mythology and folk history are rich in descriptive detail concerning the misdeeds of witches, adding more weight to the suggestion that such belief is grounded in ancient tradition.

A tale of witch treachery current among the people of Jemez Pueblo is always related as having taken place "in the beginning." Then, the Jemez dwelled in several villages along a stream at the foot of the Nacimiento Mountains and were prey to a band of witches (referred to as *sawish* in the Towa language of Jemez) who plotted to destroy them. Once when these evil persons met late in the night at a secret rendezvous their conversation was overheard by a young Pueblo boy. Hastening to his father, who was a native priest possessed of supernatural powers, the boy reported that the witches intended to burn the Jemez villages by wrapping pine gum in cedar bark, igniting these bundles, and casting them upon roof tops while the people slept. At once the father prepared sacred prayer sticks, and taking these, together with some clay canteens, he proceeded to a place not far from the village called Black Rocks. Here he set up the sticks in the canteens to serve as a defensive line against the inroads of witchcraft. Looking up from his work he saw one of the neighboring pueblos ablaze and the fire sweeping out of control directly toward him. But when the flames reached Black Rocks the prayer sticks went into action, spewing out streams of water and quenching the fire. The other pueblos, lacking this protection, were all destroyed, and only those Indians who escaped to the river were saved. For that reason, according to popular Jemez belief, only one of their pueblos exists today, and it continues to be bedeviled by witches in its midst who seek to complete the ruin of their predecessors.[6]

A figure common in Pueblo folk tales is Coyote, the arch trickster, who receives blame for introducing witchcraft among the Indians. According to a Tewa story, Coyote married Yellow Corn Girl and taught her how to change herself into an animal by leaping through a ring. Following this transformation she and Coyote slew her mother and brother by witchcraft, and from that point on witches have plied their iniquitous trade along the Rio Grande. Several elements of this tale — metamorphosis into an animal, passing through a ring, and the Coyote figure — are features that recur again and again in southwestern witchcraft lore, both Indian and Spanish.

Before discussing the theory and practice of Pueblo witchcraft, some mention must be made of religion and the Indian's view of the natural and spiritual worlds. Although each of the thirty or more pueblos existing today possesses its own set of beliefs and ceremonial patterns, enough uniformity may be found to justify describing in generalities the principal features of religious custom and activity.

Unlike some Indian groups elsewhere in North America, the Pueblos adhere to no belief in a single anthropomorphic, supreme being or great spirit. For them a universal spirit permeates the world, even inanimate objects. By the use of carefully ordered prayers and rituals, this cosmic spirit may be influenced for man's benefit; but, conversely, evil forces may also be activated by persons familiar with proper procedures and secret formulas. In thus assigning spiritual qualities to objects and forces in nature, the religion might best be described as formal animism.

Traditionally a hierarchy of native priests, led by a *cacique* or "head priest," directs all phases of village life, acting through clans or medicine societies. In the Pueblos' own view of their society, the priest maintains a special relationship with a pantheon of personalized gods, who bring blessings upon the people. At the other pole stands the witch who personifies evil and whose dark machinations continuously tilt individuals or the tribe toward disaster. In actual fact, the concept of evil in Pueblo religion is poorly defined — certainly it lacks the precise delineation found in Christianity — and as a result witchcraft provides a convenient vehicle for explaining situations and human activities that run counter to the normal course of events.[7]

Both native priest and witch are powerful figures cast in antithetical roles, each favored by possession of extraordinary knowledge. The motives of witches are directed toward benefiting themselves, whereas Pueblo ethics affirm that the highest good comes from mutual cooperation and sharing and that supernatural knowledge should be directed toward improvement of the world at large. As will be illustrated later, persons who excel in any endeavor or become conspicuously rich may come under suspicion as witches since to all appearances their energies are directed toward personal aggrandizement rather than the common good.

The struggle to overcome the injurious effects of witchcraft has been institutionalized among the Pueblos in their highly specialized curing societies, although the village cacique because of his esoteric knowledge may at times act alone to exorcise witches. Belief prevails that representatives of good inevitably triumph, but their victory comes neither easily nor swiftly. Thus practitioners of a curing society must expend considerable effort and time and demonstrate exceptional courage when they agree to treat a person suffering from bewitchment. Since witches may cause illness in two ways, either stealing the heart (soul) of the victim or shooting objects into his body, the societies, to produce a cure, must suck the objects from the body or retrieve the heart by engaging the evil thieves in combat.

In the Keresan Pueblos, medicine men of the healing society paint their faces red and black and, dressed only in a breechcloth, appear at the patient's bedside to smoke, sing, pray, mix sacred matter in a bowl, and massage the body after rubbing their hands with ashes. When they discover some foreign object, they suck it out and spit it into a clay bowl. If the doctors conclude the heart has been stolen by witches, they announce their intention to find and retrieve it. To accomplish this they leave the sick chamber armed with flint knives and bear amulets for protection and disappear in the darkness. If forced to travel far, the medicine men may leave the ground and fly through the air. Once the witches are discovered a momentous battle ensues and occasionally the evil ones temporarily get the upper hand. In such cases, they overpower their opponents by blowing a foul breath in their faces and then tying them up with baling wire. If the doctors are having a bad time of it in the fight, they are allowed to seek refuge in the nearest church to renew their strength. Usually, though, they emerge victorious, capture a witch, and take him home where he is shot full of arrows by the war chief. As evidence of their fierce struggle their bodies may be smeared with blood or soot. With the witch, the medicine men bring back the lost heart, often in the form of a ball of rags containing a grain of corn in the center. The patient is given this grain to swallow and forthwith recovers his health. At the conclusion of the ceremony, the exhausted practitioners are given food (chile stew, bread, and coffee) and baskets of cornmeal by the patient's relatives as payment for their services.[8]

The elaborate rituals as well as mock battles engaged in by the curing societies serve quite effectively to allay anxiety and promote a "cure" among persons suffering mental distress, particularly when they firmly believe their condition is caused by a witch. The elaborate shock treatment, so artfully contrived, attacks the root of bewitchment, eliminates it, and, at least briefly, restores the patient. Unfortunately within Pueblo cosmology there is no provision for final defeat of witches, so that a person cured by ceremony gains no immunity.[9]

An elaborate pattern of beliefs associated with witches' deeds is shared by all southwestern village Indians, although significant variations may be discerned among the several language groups or even within individual pueblos. In broad terms, all are concerned with witchcraft as the cause of sickness, weather adversity, or any calamity that threatens tribal welfare, and with the identification and extermination of witches. It would be no exaggeration to declare that the Pueblos are obsessively preoccupied with the threat posed by adherents to the black craft and that this fear is endemic, occasionally breaking forth even today, as in the past, in witch scares or crazes that may convulse an entire village.

Two widely separate pueblos, those of Nambé and Zuñi, have been particularly susceptible to witch mania, and the traumas they have suffered in succumbing to this affliction will be described in some detail in chapters that follow. But other villages have experienced serious internal dislocations no less severe nor less damaging to the psychic and physical well-being of their inhabitants. According to early sources, the Pueblo of Zia declined sharply in population toward the end of the seventeenth century because excessive witch phobia resulted in an inordinate number of executions. For similar reason, the Tewa community of Santa Clara dwindled in size during the last years of the Spanish colonial period. And at least one scholar has stated that the Hopi pueblo of Awatobi was destroyed in 1700 and its male inhabitants massacred by the other Hopi because of the village's dedication to witchcraft.[10]

The malevolent actions of Pueblo witches are manifested in a variety of ways, but to the Indians the most common activity of such persons is that relating to sickness and death. When people become ill, if the real cause is not immediately apparent, witchcraft ordinarily receives full blame. The ailing victim has deliberately or inadvertently offended a witch and the illness has been meted out as his punishment. In some cases the malady may be diagnosed as "loss of the heart or soul," and, as described above, members of the curing society will be summoned to perform ritually a recovery of the stolen part. Far more commonly, the disease is thought to follow magical injection of some foreign object into the body such as a thorn, stick, splinter of bone, piece of sharp glass, or even an insect or snake. Often the witch achieves this injec-

PLATE 3. *A Zuñi man, accused of witchcraft, 1895. (George Wharton James photograph)*

tion through use of a doll or image. A clay figure made from earth upon which the victim has urinated is especially potent. Using prickly pear spines or any other pointed article, the witch pierces those parts of the image in which he wishes to cause pain in the person.

Dolls of deer hide, cloth, or wool are also made. They are given the name of the party to be injured, and are then punctured with a thorn or other object. In this sinister work, the image may sometimes be smeared with the blood of a coyote or snake. A lingering illness, one that does not yield to the usual herbal remedies known by the people of the Rio Grande, will sooner or later be classed as a case of bewitchment, and a plea for aid brings the medicine man. The doctors among some pueblos waved eagle wing feathers over the body of the patient to purify it and locate the sharp particle that had penetrated the vital organs. The eagle is considered good medicine because he soars high over the earth and has eyes strong enough to see small things far below. Parts of the bear also figured prominently in many curing ceremonies. For example, the skin of a bear's leg with the claws attached was slipped over the arm of a practitioner who struck forceful blows on his patient's back and chest chasing out pockets of evil and imparting strength and long life. Some medicine men implored the assistance of badgers since by burrowing underground they could locate buried witch bundles.[11]

As indicated, sucking out a foreign object is a standard procedure in the medicine kit of all native healers. At Acoma Pueblo a number of years ago, according to an Indian witness, a priest had sucked and swallowed several things from a patient's body, but for some reason was unable to vomit them up again and was seized with terrible pain. A fellow medicine man came to his aid and laid the sick doctor on his back. With a large flint knife he cut him open, the incision running in a line down his thorax and abdomen. Those standing around could see the heart, stomach, and other internal parts. The doctor probed inside and found a big ball of cactus thorns, which he threw into the refuse bowl. Then he closed the grisly incision, rubbed the flint over it, clapped his hands and blew on it, and all was as before. The spectators could not discern where the cut had been made. Then the fellow who had swallowed the thorns got up and went about his work.[12]

As a rule anyone bewitched will die unless powerful forces can be brought to play to counteract the evil that has been done. Formerly among all southwestern Indian groups, a list of individuals whose deaths were attributed to witchcraft could be assembled by any student who cared to compile such a grim roll. Today, although young people give less credence to the efficacy of the black arts, many older Indians firmly believe that witches continue to ply their evil trade and carry away friends and relatives.

It should be noted that the Pueblos ascribe death by supernatural causes not only to witches but also to the phenomenon known as the "death scare." An example of this arose in the 1930s when archeological excavations were being conducted at the Puyé Ruins on a mesa northwest of Santa Fe. In the course of the work, some men from nearby San Ildefonso Pueblo were employed to aid in the digging, and according to stories that became current they were frequently assaulted by skeletons they uncovered. One Indian was digging when something seized his foot and called, "Don't take me from this ground." The terrified fellow yelled, "I don't know who is talking to me underground," and shortly afterward he became sick and died. Bones talked to other workers pleading "Don't take me out," but the excavation continued since the San Ildefonsos were making good wages. However, the entire pueblo paid for this folly when many people subsequently died.[13]

Not only individual sickness but epidemic disease is imputed to witchcraft. Plague or mass illness is always looked upon with particular horror since it threatens the existence of the entire tribe; and, as a consequence, during such times of stress a frenetic search for witches may end in considerable bloodletting. Although colonial records are not conclusive on this point, it is plausible to suggest that the numerous and virulent epidemics that swept across the Southwest during the Spanish period were inevitably followed by witchcraft trials and executions among the Pueblos and perhaps among the superstition-ridden European settlers as well. The same might have ensued after destruction of crops by plagues of caterpillars or grasshoppers, since these insects were regarded as agents of witches.

An instance of an epidemic ascribed to witchcraft in the twentieth century has been recorded for the Pueblo of Acoma. According to the details learned by an anthropologist, whooping cough broke out in the village. Late at night the people heard a man parading through the streets beating a drum, the muted notes sounding like a person coughing. This remarkable occurrence served as clear evidence that a witch had introduced the epidemic, and the medicine societies called a hasty meeting to determine what should be done. In an effort to identify the guilty party, they put up a special altar and laid upon it sacred paraphernalia, including a *ma-caiyoyo* or "rock crystal" which gives second sight. Using this they located the witch, and fortified with bear paws and flint knives they went out to capture him while the population of Acoma waited in suspense.

About three miles west of the pueblo, the medicine men discovered a horse named Bessie, fully saddled and bridled, that was well known to them. The animal belonged to a boy then attending the Indian School in Albuquerque. Not far away they seized the "witch man" himself and carried him back as a prisoner to the underground religious house or kiva. The people waiting inside this chamber heard a struggle on the roof and saw the feet and legs of the witch as he was pushed below. When he had descended as far as his waist, the man turned into a rat, dropped to the floor, and began scurrying around the room. The medicine men leaped on the loathsome creature, killing it and throwing the body into the fireplace. They then announced the name of the witch: the young Acoma lad away in Albuquerque at school.

On the following day the government agent for the pueblo received a telephone message saying that the same boy had killed himself the previous night by leaping from a window on the third floor of his dormitory. For the Indians this news confirmed the identification made by their medicine men, and when the boy's body was returned for burial they refused him a place in the church cemetery because he was a witch and responsible for the epidemic.[14]

One of the most serious catastrophes of modern times which was attributed to the intervention of witches was the great influenza epidemic of 1918. All southwestern Indian villages were filled with the sick and dying, and church bells tolled incessantly for those already departed. In Isleta a special ceremony was conducted by the medicine men to drive out the witches responsible for the disease, but it had little effect. The cacique claimed to have found a bundle of shredded rattlesnakes and coyote hair hanging in a tree near the road to the village cemetery. This witch bundle laughed day and night and made fun of persons passing by who carried dead relatives to their graves. The witch owning the bundle made everyone die so he could enjoy the funerals.[15]

Another supernatural explanation of plagues and epidemics is that they represent a game played by witches in human lives. A well-circulated tale among the Indians concerns a conclave of witches which met secretly at night to gamble in human hearts. The losing side spreads disease among innocent villagers and with the souls of those who perish the debts are paid.[16]

In the early 1920s a Pueblo woman, well known as a potter, declared that of her twelve children, nine had died as a result of witchcraft. She stated they had been bewitched by some of her Spanish-American neighbors who were envious of her success in pottery making. According to her accusation, because of this jealousy they had caused the deaths of her babies by breaking eggs over their heads when she was not around. It is widely held among the Indians that a particular portion of the egg white is bewitched and that when it touches the soft spot of a baby's head, the infant begins to sicken and soon dies.[17]

What exactly motivates Pueblo witches to go about their nefarious trade? With them there is no pact with the Devil nor any conscious self-dedication as handmaidens of evil such as appears common among notions of European witchery. Pueblo witchcraft is strongly individualistic in tone and its application generally follows upon some personal grievance, since a witch who feels an injury will retaliate. Revenge, envy, or simple spite are motives that move witches to commit harm. Jealousy, too, may cause them to persecute some innocent person. Once a good man was appointed governor of his pueblo by the council of elders and given the customary black cane as his symbol of office. The same night his family was awakened by a great commotion on the roof and realized with horror that witches were dancing over the spot where the new governor was sleeping. Apparently they frolicked with such intensity that the cane hanging on the wall shook and joined in the dance. The members of the family knew without question that this was a death ritual, and notwithstanding that the man was a tubercular, his passing that night was charged to the witches. They had been jealous of his honor.[18]

Witches, it is true, habitually wreak vengence on men, but they may also be called upon to provide love potions or charms for persons needing supernatural help in winning the attention of another. Hispano villagers residing near the pueblos and recognizing the magical power of Indian witchcraft often sought out native philters to engage the affection of someone they loved. In all probability traffic in amorous charms among Pueblo witches derived from European practice borrowed from early Spanish colonists. In the Old World, as early as the fifth century B.C., Greek poets speak of resorting to magic to bring lovers to the same bed, and witches throughout the continent traditionally supplied potions to those who requested their services. Occasionally Indian witches exercised their powers of seduction on their own behalf, as will be illustrated, in a chapter that follows on the Zuñi, by the case of a Pueblo boy who bewitched young girls for immoral purposes.

A serious aspect of the witchcraft phenomenon was the identification of practitioners. A great deal of fear was bred in the Pueblos by the fact that no one could ever be sure who might turn out to be a witch. Many Indians, prone to flights of imagination, lived in constant terror of being conjured, a state that not only affected their psychic equilibrium, but proved dangerous to all persons with whom they came in contact since they recklessly fastened their suspicions upon relatives, friends, and strangers alike. Many young mothers were particularly careful to cover their infants' faces when anyone approached, because children were believed to be the special targets of witches. A man of Isleta Pueblo refused to allow visitors to enter his house, so timorous was he that one might prove to be a witch in disguise.

Witches, in the Pueblo view, are most apt to be persons living in your own village or even in your own household. Apprehension over suspicious conduct of relatives abounds at Zuñi and other places. Even medicine men may come under a cloud if their conduct deviates the slightest degree from the accepted norm. It is freely acknowledged that disciples of the black arts are as common among Hispano neighbors as among the Indians themselves, but there is no general agreement on the incidence of witchcraft among Anglos. Except for anthropologists, whose probing into village affairs makes them suspect, the White community is thought to contain few if any witches, primarily because it places no faith in the craft.

Given all the uncertainty, most Pueblos are exceedingly careful to be courteous to everyone they meet, whatever their origin, lest they unwittingly offend a witch and provoke trouble. Father Noel Dumarest, writing in the early part of this century, suggested that the social timidity of these Indians was closely connected to their witchcraft theories. He wrote, "Why are the Pueblos so pacific? Why do they not try even to defend themselves in quarrels? Because from their youth their elders have taught them that nobody can know the hearts of men. There are witches everywhere."[19]

The non-Pueblo Pima of southern Arizona established a way to ferret out witches: they buried feathered wands in the desert and whoever accidentally found them was immediately branded a witch. However, among the Rio Grande villagers there was no single well-defined method for exposing evildoers. Certain categories of individuals were acutely vulnerable to accusations of witchcraft. These included old women and even men, particularly if they happened to be senile or otherwise ravaged by age; anyone with a physical deformity; persons careless in their speech, dishonest, or possessed of wealth from unknown sources; anyone who had made an enemy of a prominent member of the tribe; and people who went prowling about the village late at night peering into windows. Lurking about a house where someone is ill invites suspicion, and homes of invalids as a matter of course are kept under surveillance in order to trap witches responsible for causing the sickness.

It is not unusual for persons to gain reputations for being witches and yet live for long periods unmolested. Their neighbors, nevertheless, regard them with circumspection and take pains to stay on their good side. For many years a couple resided at Isleta, the man from San Felipe and his wife a Laguna, who were generally conceded to be witches, but though much whispering was done no serious charge was ever filed against them. While decisive action may never be taken against such suspected parties they are shunned as discreetly as possible without being offered overt offense.

If some untoward event occurs and blame needs to be fixed, medicine men may have recourse to obsidian (black volcanic glass) or rock crystal, gazing into these for purposes of divination. Normally, though, an accusation of witchcraft by a victim is quite enough in itself to establish the identity of a witch and, if a crime has been committed, to bring him to trial. In a few pueblos charges may be constantly and incautiously bandied about, but only should a bewitchment result in serious illness or death does a trial and punishment of a witch ensue.

At Cochití Pueblo if a person is suspected of witchcraft he is taken before the war captain by the accuser who tells what he knows or has seen. Damaging evidence includes climbing on roof tops and peering down chimneys or through windows, and throwing dirt or cornmeal into the Rio Grande where witches are supposed to live. The accused may be dragged to one of the society houses and held under close guard until he confesses. No force is used, but he is denied food, and within time, because of sheer weariness, comes out with a confession. On occasion death has resulted due to fatigue or exhaustion. This judicial process has not been used in recent years because no one at Cochití has been charged with a major crime of witchcraft.[20]

All Pueblos probably executed witches at one time, although the practice declined after 1900 as pressure was applied by the United States government. The trial system and method of execution practiced by the Zuñi are best known, as later discussion will reveal, but variations in procedure could be found throughout the Southwest. The Yumas and Mojaves dwelling near the Colorado River punished witches, who always happened to be women, by drawing them up by the hands until they confessed. Once the confession had been extracted, they were killed.[21] Even though these people were not Pueblo, it is possible they borrowed this technique of treating witches from their village neighbors on the east. At Isleta the customary treatment for a captured witch was to place him in a squatting position, keeping him there and replacing him when he fell over, until he died.[22] In the early 1880s two witches were clubbed to death at Zia. Executing a witch nullified his evil power and released victims from spells under which they suffered. Since capital punishment is now frowned upon, witch baiting has declined in importance with the result that greater weight is presently given to the extraction of foreign objects.

Indictments of witchcraft are, as a rule, pinned upon individuals, but the Indians acknowledge that an evil strain may affect an entire family so that the black arts are passed on from one generation to the next. A common saying among the Southern Tewa in the vicinity of Albuquerque is that "If a woman is not right," in other words a witch, "her children get it." In years past, accusations of witchcraft have led entire families to flee their pueblo to escape the wrath of their neighbors.

Another method of acquiring competence in the witch's arts, other than inheriting the familial tradition, is to purchase power from anyone who has it and is willing to sell. The price consists of an initial sum ($30 in one reported instance) plus a later fee of which the buyer is often unaware. One Pueblo youth bought supernatural power to make him a successful pitcher in baseball games and another to make him irresistible to women. The deferred payment may be called in months or even years after the original bargain, when the seller demands that his client sacrifice, or bewitch, some close relative. If he refuses, a spell falls upon him and he dies.[23]

In a few places the Indians believe witches have organized themselves in a society under their own officers. This feature is vaguely reminiscent of the European covens or underground cells of witches composed of twelve members and a leader. According to information from Laguna Pueblo, witch society members are bound to the orders of their officers, and, when bidden, they must go out and make people sick. To be initiated a candidate is obliged to sacrifice or bewitch someone to death.[24] At Isleta whenever the medicine societies initiate a new member, the local lodge of witches feels compelled to follow suit so that their special enemies will not get an edge upon them. If they cannot find anyone willing to join, they may exhume from the graveyard someone whose death they recently caused and initiate him.[25]

Among some of the Keresan villages a likely prospect may be offered special inducements over a long period of time in

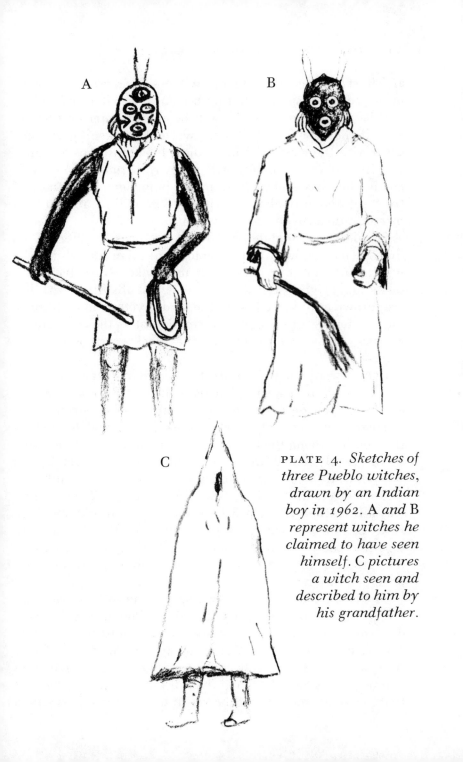

PLATE 4. *Sketches of three Pueblo witches, drawn by an Indian boy in 1962. A and B represent witches he claimed to have seen himself. C pictures a witch seen and described to him by his grandfather.*

an effort to woo him into the witches' society. He may be promised, for instance, that by becoming a witch his powers will be vastly expanded: he will be able to enter any house, even if the door is locked, and, without awakening anyone, sleep with the woman of his choice; his abilities as a hunter will increase and the deer will never run from him; he will be able to speak and understand all languages, even those of the birds and animals; and with ease he will be able to turn himself into a coyote, crow, owl, or deer.

Should the candidate be seduced by this rich offering, he then is led through a protracted initiation in which the witches attempt to frighten him and shake his resolve. He is taken to a brightly lighted cave, where skulls filled with fire are thrown at him, snakes writhe, and coyotes and owls make hideous noises. In the end he formally enters the company of witches, and occult secrets of the black craft become his possession.[26]

Lycanthropy, or the ability to change oneself into a wolf and back again, is a conspicuous feature of European witchery. From this derived the popular superstition, strongest in Germany, of werewolves who killed people and feasted on their flesh. Among the Pueblos, belief in animal metamorphosis was firmly rooted. In assuming the shape of beasts, Indian witches could more easily go about their wicked pursuits and escape detection. Yet there was danger too, for if the animal was killed, the evil turned back on the witch and she died. Elsie C. Parsons, who was well-versed in Pueblo customs, says that the belief that wounding or killing the witch animal produces the same effect in the witch person is of European derivation.[27]

The forms that a witch may assume tend to vary from one village to another. At Santo Domingo Pueblo it may be a dog, coyote, or owl; at San Felipe, an owl; at Cochití, a crow, coyote, bear, or wolf; at Zia, a donkey or rat; and at Santa Ana, an owl, dog, coyote, or a tiny figure of a man with feathers in his hair.[28] Among the Zuñi there is a story current that a witchwoman turned herself into a deer using as an aid ear wax from that animal.[29] The domestic cat, on account of its stealthy habits and fondness for roaming at night, is a form often taken by witches. Indeed, the association of witches and cats is almost worldwide and its presence even among the Pueblos is not surprising.

The following story related by a young Zuñi mother attests to the dread that may be inspired by any unusual behavior of cats.

> I was sleeping alone in the large upper room. My brother slept on the roof nearby. I was awakened by the approach of a creature like a large cat; but it was not a cat; I knew at once that it was a witch. It came close to my bed and looked at my little one, and then hastened from the room. It went out through the broken window pane. In a short time my baby died.[30]

Regarding snakes and their relation to witchcraft, some ambivalence exists among the Indians. The Hopi Pueblos of northern Arizona look upon snakes as brothers of men, and serpents of all kinds are used to carry messages to the gods. In their famous snake dances, native priests handle and charm deadly rattlesnakes and release them in the four directions. Ceremonies involving ritual use of reptiles were also present among the Rio Grande pueblos when the Spaniards first arrived, but because of intense pressure applied by the Franciscan missionaries they were soon abandoned. In fact the eastern villages seem to have been won over, at least partially, to the Spanish view that snakes were loathsome creatures, the servants of evil, and the accomplices of witches. Thus when snakes were found in the home, they were not only killed but burned to vitiate any harm they might have caused. Notwithstanding, some medicine men believed it possible to turn the great power of rattlesnakes to positive purposes to benefit the entire tribe. The persistent legend of a guardian snake kept by now extinct Pecos Pueblo will be related in a succeeding chapter.

A curious incident involving a snake is related by anthropologist Esther Goldfrank who did field work at Cochití in the 1920s. A large flat-bottomed boat was used by the Indians as a ferry to cross the Rio Grande to their fields on the east side of the river. One day it overturned on a stump in midstream, and the following morning a red snake was seen coming out of the same stump. The people unanimously concurred that this was the witch who had caused the boat disaster.[31]

A representative story from the Pueblos illustrates the kind of action that may be taken when a witch animal menaces the welfare of a community. In this case an epidemic had struck the village and people were dying in large numbers. The council of priests and elders convened and decided that the disease was brought by some unidentified witch who had become an implacable enemy of the pueblo. Further, the council concluded that the only way to catch the culprit was to snare him while he was parading as a predatory beast. No suspicious animal had been seen near the village, so it was agreed he must approach by an arroyo which skirted the houses and fields and formed the only secret entry.

Accordingly it was decided to set a trap, but this proved impossible since no one knew what kind of animal form the witch had donned. Therefore the council ruled that a man should be stationed in the arroyo to seize the witch when it passed by, and lots were cast to choose someone for the unlucky post. The grave situation demanded extreme measures and the newly selected witchcatcher was starved for many days until he resembled a skeleton. In the meanwhile a dog was killed and allowed to decay, and the emaciated man was smeared with the putrid flesh. That night he lay down in the arroyo while sentinels hid in the chamisa above.

As predicted, the witch appeared. A coyote came creeping down the dry stream bed and when he observed the prone man he drew back. But catching the odor of death, he approached again. The man threw his arms around the animal and held on fiercely until his fellow tribesmen came to the rescue and killed the coyote. All expectations were confirmed.

When the beast was cut open, its stomach was found to be filled with cactus thorns, the food of witches. The heart was promptly burned to destroy the malefactor's power, and almost at once the epidemic ceased and misery was banished from the village.[32]

From Isleta Pueblo comes a dark tale of witchery showing a somewhat different use of animal metamorphosis. In this instance an innocent boy is changed into a coyote by an enemy but eventually escapes his fate and sees retribution visited upon the witch.

Once an old Isleta woman lived with and cared for her grandson who was her sole means of support. The boy was a superb hunter and kept his grandmother's table well supplied with venison. A neighbor, who was secretly envious of the lad's skill with a rifle, often came to visit, and one evening he said, "My friend, how do you get deer? I go out and get none."

"It is easy to kill deer," the boy replied. "Let us go hunting together tomorrow." So they agreed and set out.

Reaching the pine-clad Manzano Mountains, they made camp and in the morning started to hunt in different directions. The boy traveled north, found his deer, killed and butchered it, and brought it to camp. The man as usual had no luck and returned empty-handed. Even though his young companion offered him half his deer, he was filled with resentment, and the next morning he said, "My friend, let us play a game."

They sat down on a blanket and the man displayed a fine woven belt rolled in a tight knot. "Try your luck," he said. "If you can catch the fringe the belt is yours." Then he unrolled it, and when the boy caught the fringe at the end he turned into a coyote.

Chuckling, the man packed the entire deer on a donkey they had brought, and as the coyote began to cry he said in parting, "Good-by my friend. I am going. All this mountain is yours. Try hard and you will get a rabbit to eat."

When he got home his wife asked him what had become of

his partner. And he replied, "I do not know anything about him. We separated in the mountains and I went one way and he the other." Later when the old grandmother came to inquire he repeated the same story.

Five days later the boy appeared at his grandmother's house as a coyote and began sleeping under the ladder that led to the upper floor. Village dogs barked at him but kept their distance knowing that he was really a person. People began wondering if the coyote was hanging around waiting for an opportunity to kill chickens, so they chased him away.

The coyote fled and approached a camp where two men were herding sheep. Since their dogs refused to attack, the herders judged that this was a good coyote and they threw him some bones. Seeing the poor beast crying, they drew near and asked if he was really a person that had been bewitched. They put the same question three times and at each the coyote nodded yes. Then they wrapped him in a sheepskin, placd him on their donkey and carried him to the village war chief. The medicine men were called and they began to ask the coyote if he was a person. Again he cried and nodded his head.

After four days of fasting, the medicine men prepared a ceremony and fashioned a ring of sticks. Sprinkling sacred water on the coyote, they instructed him to leap through the ring, and as he did he became the boy once more. Then he told the elders the whole story of his bewitchment. When he finished, they gave him a small ring and explained how to use it in attaining vengeance.

No sooner did he reach his grandmother's house than the man came running, having learned of the boy's return. "Well, my friend, have you come back?" he said.

"Yes, I was visiting in another village all this time," the boy answered. "Let us go hunting again, and perhaps this time you will get something." And the man foolishly accepted.

They camped as before in the mountains, and the boy produced the ring saying, "While we are resting, let us play a game. You jump through this ring and you can have it."

No sooner had the man leaped through than he turned into a rattlesnake. As the boy loaded the donkey, he advised the defeated witch, "If you are lucky your sons will come and feed you, but if not you will have nothing and better stay hidden under the rocks." And he left the rattlesnake alone.[33]

Transformation by passing through a ring is a pervasive element in southwestern witchcraft lore. Many Indians are convinced that by going through a magic hoop or artificial rainbow, witches change themselves into various animals and birds, and it is in this state that they may be most easily captured and destroyed. The Laguna people maintain that placing a loop of twisted yucca fibers on the head allows a person to assume any form he desires.[34] A professed Zuñi witch declared that by jumping through a hoop of yucca, he could make himself into a dog, cat, coyote, hawk, crow, or owl for the purpose of passing quickly and in disguise about the country.[35]

Almost without exception the several Pueblo groups associate owls and crows with witchery and spellbinding. Members of the Keresan villages carefully avoid contact with the feathers of either bird for this reason. At Cochití a man heard two owls calling and recognized the voices of persons he knew. His son chased the birds away by firing a bullet marked with a cross in the air.[36] At the same pueblo some crows once threw rocks at a house where five men were sick. When two of the men died, it was known witches were masquerading as the crows.[37]

Another conviction shared by the Pueblos is that witches may manifest their presence at night by appearing as flashes of light. Taos and Laguna people credit witches with being able to travel as balls of fire. The Cochití describe such enchanted fireballs as measuring six to twelve inches in diameter and consisting of a black center with a surrounding surface of fiery, red flames.[38] Indians of San Juan speak of witches "walking as fire."[39] The Southern Tewa explain that strange lights perceived in the night are likely to be flying witches on some noxious errand. As a result of this belief, when the Isletas saw their first train locomotive with its flashing lights they identified it as an agent of witchcraft.[40] A light which is seen and vanishes suddenly is interpreted by both the Laguna and Zuñi as an omen of death for some loved one.

A man at Cochití once reported that his wife saw two balls of fire come out of the chimney of the house next door. They rolled about the roof, then fell to the ground and into the plaza. The next night he went to watch and the same thing occurred. He wanted to catch the fireballs but his wife and cousins held him back. Soon the balls turned to ashes, like burned rags, and as he kicked them they fell to pieces. Describing this unusual performance to the village cacique, the man was advised that the next time he saw the balls he should grab a handful of the ashes. Then on the following day he should look closely and see if any man had a tear or hole in his trousers or a woman a hole in her dress. In this way he would know who were the witches.[41]

Since witches shun the company of virtuous men, they love the night and lurk in shadows and darkness where their activities may go undetected. For this reason their favorite rendezvous is a cave. Other tribes, including the Navajo and the Opata of Sonora, also believe witches haunt the black void of caverns. According to Pueblo tradition, Indians of Sandía once had a settlement at a place called *Shimtua* which was located adjacent to a cave where witches assembled. Sandía today, situated just north of Albuquerque, is still considered a haven for witches by some persons who refuse to visit the village.[42]

In spite of what has just been said, information on Pueblo witchcraft is more uncertain and in smaller supply than is the case for most other aspects of the culture. This is easily understood when it is realized that the Indians are loath to discuss the subject in any detail for fear that supernatural powers may somehow retaliate. Many Pueblos deny that witchcraft is still practiced today, or that people continue to believe in it. Others will admit that it existed in the past and that some people died, and a few will tell what they claim to have heard secondhand about witchcraft in another village. In rare instances, this writer, as well as other investigators, has been told of incidents which the informant claimed to have experienced himself. But in the end, our knowledge of the nature and practice of witchcraft among the Pueblos must remain sketchy and incomplete.

6

The Tragedy of Nambé

THE WIND OF EARLY SPRING creeping down from the high peaks above Santa Fe still contained enough of winter's chill so the motley assortment of Indians, Mexicans, and Anglo-Americans crowding the old plaza pulled serapes or buffalo hide coats tighter about their bodies. It was a March evening, 1854, less than a decade after the United States had seized the Southwest from Mexico, and the New Mexico Territorial Court was in session. In a room dimly lit by candles, within the mud walls of the venerable Governor's Palace, the Honorable Grafton Baker, Chief Justice, presided. Not everyone in the curious throng had been able to find a place in the tightly packed courtroom, and the overflow had spilled into the adobe square outside. The case under consideration and exciting such interest was that of four Nambé Indians, accused of executing two of their fellow tribesmen for witchcraft.

According to the story pieced together from numerous accusations, the two murdered men, Luís Romero and Antonio Tafolla, had been practicing witches who devoured children of their village, witnesses having seen them pull bones of the victims from their mouths and noses. A council of all the people had been called, evidence presented, and the death penalty pronounced. Thereupon the executioners were named and they went out of the pueblo at dusk with the two condemned men who were made to kneel side by side and were then felled by a single shotgun blast to the head.

96

Upon word of the incident, the new territorial authorities arrested the four Indians actually involved in the killing, although it was apparent the entire village was implicated. The matter had aroused some consternation among the native populace, both Indian and Spanish, because it could not be understood why anyone would object to the removal of dangerous witches from a community. The officers of Nambé, speaking through court interpreters, explained that having full jurisdiction to administer the internal affairs of the pueblo, they considered it their duty to search out evildoers and inflict appropriate punishment. That they had this authority was not challenged. The issue concerning the court was whether witchcraft actually existed and could be considered a crime under the law.

The most important person to testify was the Indian governor of Nambé, Juan Ignacio Tapolla, who unhesitatingly admitted that by common assent the two witches had been done away with in the manner described. Part of his testimony ran as follows:

> The four defendants came and reported to me that they had killed Luís Romero and Antonio Tafolla, in accordance with the order of the pueblo. It was done in the beginning of this month. They only said they had killed them; I did not see them after they were killed. They were killed at twilight not quite a league from the pueblo, in a north direction. I saw them going out with the deceased; they had a shotgun. Juan Diego carried the gun. I saw them when they came back to report to me. They were killed by order of the pueblo and the head men of the pueblo. I am the governor of the pueblo, and Juan Diego is the *fiscal* ["constable"]. It was the duty of the *fiscal* to execute the orders of the pueblo. They commanded him to kill these two men. The bad acts spoken of were that they were detected in the act of witchcraft and sorcery: they had eaten up the little children of the pueblo. It has always been our custom to put

a stop to and check bad acts. We have not exercised this custom of killing witches since the Americans came here, because there had not been such doings before. This act was done by the command of myself and the whole pueblo.[1]

Justice Baker in all his judicial career had never confronted a case such as this. Perhaps through his mind passed scenes of Salem and the realization that history might treat him harshly if he failed to act with scrupulous care. In any event, he finally decided to side-step the whole issue. Because the venue was not clearly proved, the crime having occurred upon or near the line between two counties, he announced that the prisoners were discharged and the case was closed. For the four Indians of Nambé, who had originally pleaded not guilty, the release was interpreted as a vindication of their actions. The skeptical Ameicans, it seemed, really hated witches as much as their Spanish predecessors.

The old Pueblo of Nambé rests in a narrow valley, bestride a crystalline stream of the same name, seven leagues northeast of Santa Fe. Surrounding it the country is seamed and eroded by little canyons and arroyos that have cut grotesque shapes in the red soil and sandstone. On the east rises the darkly timbered wall of the Blood of Christ Mountains, the Sangre de Cristo, where the Rio Nambé that passes through the pueblo before joining the Rio Grande has its headwaters. Neat fields of alfalfa, chile, corn, and pumpkin encircle the village and patriarchal cottonwoods with massive trunks and arms offer a welcome umbrella of shade to Indian farmers on a midsummer's day. Altogether it is an idyllic corner of the Southwest, far removed from the giddy, fast-paced life that typifies most of twentieth-century America. And yet as the witchcraft case cited above suggests, things have not always been so serene for the people of Nambé.

The historical record points to several Rio Grande villages, Santa Clara, Zia, Sandía, Santa Ana, Nambé, as having experienced disastrous episodes of witch mania. Indeed it is suspected that the severity of these resulted in significant population decline because of the large number of executions. Against Tewa-speaking Nambé has this charge been most consistently leveled, and the evidence of both history and folk tradition seems to bear out the indictment.

A tale still current among these Indians in the 1920s referred to an unhappy experience suffered by the pueblo during the seventeenth century. A new priest, sent by the Spanish Church to minister to the village, was an unbending disciplinarian, intolerant of the ancient ceremonial dances, and determined to root out all vestiges of paganism. The Indians petitioned him for restraint, but the haughty friar turned a deaf ear and denounced the native rituals as witchcraft and the cacique, or head priest, as a wizard. Summoning soldiers from Santa Fe to assist in his unholy crusade, he sent them into the Indian kiva, the most sacred religious chamber, and had all the village's ceremonial objects carried to the plaza for burning. As a final blow he ordered the arrest of Táhwi, the aged cacique, and saw him taken in fetters to Santa Fe for a trial as a witch.

The priest himself journeyed to the capital to present testimony against Táhwi. He declared the cacique had bewitched him so he was prevented from sleeping at night, and when he said Mass sharp pains pierced his back. Also, he asserted piously, this fiend had bewitched other Indians so they refused to come for services. Táhwi stoutly denied he had bewitched anyone, but the weight of his accuser's claims overrode his objections and he was put to the torture — not by the Church, but by civil authorities as was the custom. The cacique's hands were tied behind him and he was suspended by the thumbs. Suffering from excruciating pain, he finally confessed to taking holy water from the church and attempting to work magic with it. On the basis of this confession he was convicted and hanged, along with another cacique from the Pueblo of San Ildefonso, condemned on a similar charge.[2]

This incident quite likely took place in the 1670s during

the period of intense friction between Spaniard and Pueblo and just prior to the great Indian revolt of 1680 that has been described in an earlier chapter. As already noted, the friars of this era were obsessed with the notion that Indian witches labored full time to undo the program of evangelization, and to bring sickness or death upon them. Apparently the cleric of Nambé was among those most sorely affected by the virus of superstition, and he may have suffered retribution if he was the Fray Tomás listed in the Spanish documents as the priest slain at Nambé on August 10, 1680.

Although the Táhwi affair took place at a relatively early date, it cannot be assumed that witchcraft had already seized hold of the minds of the Nambés. In fact when a more en-lightened priest, Fray Atanasio Domínguez, visited the place a century later in 1776, far from picturing its inhabitants as witch-ridden, he declared in his journal that "the people of this particular pueblo are docile, obedient, somewhat in-clined to goodness, and very lively and gay."[3]

The first precise archival reference to witchcraft at Nambé does not actually appear until 1822. In that year a Mexican, Gaspar Ortiz, who resided near the village made a legal dec-laration before the authorities to the effect that his nephew Santiago, then sick in bed, had been betwitched by Juan Inocencio, an Indian of Nambé. When confronted, Inocencio readily acknowledged the accusation and even admitted that he possessed the power to bring about a cure in five days. When asked in what manner he had betwitched Santiago, the Indian claimed he had gotten hold of a handful of his hair, and mixing this with feathers and cotton, he had worked his magic and caused the victim to go crazy. Accord-ing to the declaration, the self-professed witch freely con-fessed his guilt before Gaspar Ortiz, his son, and another witness, a neighbor named Antonio Quintana, as well as be-fore the council of elders of the pueblo. But if any formal penalty was assigned to Juan Inocencio, no mention of it has been preserved.[4]

In the years following this event, Nambé developed an

PLATE 5. *Kiva at Nambé Pueblo. The site of witchcraft trials in the late nineteenth century. (Museum of New Mexico photograph)*

authentic witch phobia, and by the mid-nineteenth century
it had earned an unsavory reputation throughout northern
New Mexico as a seedbed of witchery. The reasons for the
upsurge of such a phenomenon are never clear, and it is
practically impossible to say why this malignancy took root
in a small village like Nambé while neighboring pueblos
were spared any major epidemic. It is only safe to conclude
that once witch mania reached a certain level of intensity it
began snowballing with amazing rapidity until the lives of
all inhabitants were menaced and the village was faced with
extinction.

The details of Nambé's ordeal are known only sketchily,
since those intimately involved were usually unwilling to
discuss a subject so pregnant with danger. The year after
the shotgun slaying of the two alleged child-eaters, three additional men and a woman of the pueblo were "butchered
in a most horrible manner" for witchcraft crimes. Again the
executioners were brought to trial, and again they escaped
serious punishment, although they were compelled to pay
four hundred dollars, representing court costs and fees rather
than fines.[5]

In December 1883 pioneer archeologist-historian Adolph
Bandelier visited Nambé and recorded in his personal journal
several illuminating comments upon the practice of black
magic. He had already been informed by a priest at Jémez
that the Nambés were fast disappearing owing to excesses
attributed to superstition, and the writer made special efforts
to learn the nature of the problem. Although meeting the
usual reticence, he was able to say:

> I asked positively about the matter of Nambé and was
> told that they were in the habit, until 15 years ago, of
> killing their most intelligent people under the pretext of
> witchcraft, and that this has greatly contributed toward
> depopulating the pueblo. Not longer than one year ago,
> a woman at Nambé was beaten to death by order of the
> authorities for having been the concubine of a married

man. About witchcraft they know of the custom of pricking images, but have no knowledge of that of infanticides.[6]

A typical incident, probably dating from this same period, entered the Hispanic folk literature of the upper Rio Grande Valley and was related around winter hearths as late as the 1930s. In Nambé lived an Indian woman by the name of Juana Chaves who was a witch. So potent were her evil powers and so many were the subjects of her bewitchment that the people were dying out. As a result she was burned to death inside her house and nothing was left but a pile of ashes. In the foundation were discovered idols and dolls and when these too were burned, they jumped about like people. These were the agents of the old woman's witchery.[7]

In the first quarter of the twentieth century an anthropologist managed to gain the confidence of a Nambé woman and from her secured details of witch problems that disrupted the community. The informant declared that she had been condemned by relatives upon marriage to her first husband because his grandmother and her sisters, according to popular gossip, were witches. This had been subsequently borne out when the women were caught spreading a mortal sickness among the pueblo children and for their wickedness were put to death.

The event had unfolded in this way. Because the village young were dying from a cough, the chiefs and notables assembled in the kiva chamber to find a remedy. As was the custom when meetings were of long duration, women brought bowls and baskets of food, and the grandmother had been among them. She handed the chief a large basket of wafer bread and a meat bone and left. When the council sat down to eat, the medicine man "spit his medicine" around each container, and as he did this the dinner brought by the old woman began to bubble. The meat and bone were judged to be from a dead child and the woman's true identity as a witch was thereby established. None of her poison fare was touched and when she returned to reclaim her basket she found that nothing had been removed. Returning to her sisters in anger she announced, "Now they are afraid of us. We will do something bad to them."

The witch women, with a male accomplice from Tesuque Pueblo, went north of Nambé and spent a day and night preparing small dolls. In their stomachs they placed chili seeds, dirt, and rags that would cause people to cough. Once, going out, they were observed by the chief who followed their tracks and learned that at first they traveled as cats and dogs to escape detection but upon reaching a deep arroyo they changed into people again. From a hilltop the chief was able to view their devilish proceedings. The witches laughed and joked, saying, "We will put seeds in this one." The rag dolls had two faces, one face to make people sick, the other to take them to the graveyard. A large pot was simmering on the fire and inside cooked the flesh of children who had been dug from their graves.

The next night the witches returned to their grim task, but now the pueblo governor sent out his officers and arrested them. The four wretches were hauled to the deserted rectory where the priest had once lived and were bound with rawhide ropes. The eldest sister was tied with her hands behind her back and the man with his hands under his knees and a stick between. The old grandmother was in great pain and pleaded to be allowed to see her daughter, but this was refused. Then she begged, "For the love of God give this rosary to my daughter," and she handed it to the chief. But the officers took the rosary apart and between the beads found a little bag containing seeds of wheat and corn and a small stone which was the witch's bad heart. All this was thrown into the fire and as soon as it was consumed by the flames, the old woman died.

The remaining women and the man were tortured until they promised to bring no more sickness upon the pueblo, but the latter had been treated so severely that he succumbed. The women were released but not before bags containing their bad hearts were removed from their clothing. When these were later burned, they also died.[8]

Both the federal and territorial governments long neglected the southwestern pueblos and left them to their own devices, even in their handling of witchcraft crimes. But after 1900 official pressure and censure brought about a sharp decline in the number of witches killed in the Indian villages. Executions did not cease altogether for several decades and those cases that did occur were attended by the strictest secrecy. By 1910 Nambé's population had sunk to a mere eighty-eight, a consequence, most historians agree, of the tribe's elimination of suspected sorcerers, witches, and spellbinders. After this date stern penalties gradually fell into disuse, although a firm belief in witchcraft continued to promote social discord. The population today, on the increase but still small, yet carries the burden of a tragedy that once sundered the community and brought down upon it a reign of terror.

7

The Zuñi Plague of Witches

IN SEPTEMBER OF 1879 Frank Hamilton Cushing of the Bureau of American Ethnology arrived in the village of Zuñi to begin a prolonged study of Pueblo culture. At first because of his prying and note-taking, he aroused hostility among the Indians, but learning the native language, adopting the local form of dress, and taking up other customs of the people, Cushing soon ingratiated himself with important members of the community and within time received an invitation to join the sacred Bow Priesthood, the Zuñi's most important religious society.

During the summer of 1881 he accompanied a group of the Pueblo's leaders on a tour of the East, the purpose being to arouse their interest in education and broaden their view of the world. Traveling by train, the party visited Washington and was received at the White House by President Chester A. Arthur. Continuing to Boston, the Indians toured Harvard and under Cushing's guidance walked along the Atlantic beach, depositing prayer sticks and collecting water for use in ceremonials back home. High point of the trip proved to be a stop at Salem where they solemnly commended the citizenry for their ancestors' diligent persecution of witches. Zuñi, they proclaimed, still suffered from the evil effects of witchcraft and its practice was considered a capital crime. Reports of these remarks in the Boston *Herald* may well have startled New Englanders who felt little pride in the black page of history written so long before in a Salem courtroom.[1]

106

Cushing himself, during his several years residence at Zuñi, had ample opportunity to observe how deep-seated was the dread of witches among his hosts. Concentrating upon the collection of folktales and origin myths, he discovered that witchery was woven into the very fabric of Zuñi cosmology and that witches posed a daily threat for members of the community.

According to the sacred mythology, a pair of witches, male and female, ascended from the underworlds after the earth had been populated and brought with them two "gifts" to man. The first was a welcome gift of corn, the staple grain of the Indians. The witches in their travels came upon a group of Zuñi girls sitting under a ramada of piñon boughs and asked them who they were. "We are corn maidens," was the reply, "but as yet we have no corn." The witches said this was not right so they distributed seven varieties of colored Indian corn, as well as squash and melon seeds. Upon receiving the gift of crops, the maidens formed two lines facing the east in full view of the Sun Father and began to dance. Their benefactors observed approvingly throughout the night and the next day continued their migration.[2]

The second bestowal upon man made by the witches — death — was received with less enthusiasm. The underworld figures claimed this gift was necessary to prevent the earth from becoming overcrowded. Notwithstanding, man refused to view death with anything but horror, and from this grew his loathing for witches who forever remained identified as death-bringers.[3]

The tradition among the Zuñi crediting witches with dissemination of both good and evil suggests the Old World differentiation between white and black magic. The Indian view further implies that even the best of men may on occasion resort to bad practices and that use of witchcraft is not strictly limited to witches. Charges stemming from misapplication of supernatural power have been brought against pillars of the Zuñi community, and even the curing society, the principal institutional vehicle for counteracting the evils of witchery, has been known to stray into the shadowy paths of black magic. In short, a witch is one who is thoroughly dedicated to the craft as a vocation, although others may from time to time apply the occult arts to achieve some immediate goal.[4]

Anthropologist Matilda Coxe Stevenson, who pursued field work at Zuñi in the 1890s, cites the case of a highly esteemed sun priest suspected of having been responsible for a serious drought. Because of his position he escaped physical punishment but did suffer impeachment from his ceremonial office. The man selected to fill his post was far inferior in intelligence and miscalculated the winter solstice in 1894, thus throwing all the succeeding rituals off time. Although a sun priest was considered infallible in the performance of his duties, the village chiefs decided the new one had indeed made an error, and there was some regret that the old priest had been condemned as a witch since his calculations had always been without blemish.[5]

Imbedded in the oral folk traditions of Zuñi is the theme of witchcraft, usually represented in tales of adversity. One familiar story concerns a youth who was in the habit of visiting and showing attention to a pair of sisters, unaware that one of them was a witch. He finally fell in love with the good sister, married her and they lived together in the village. Each day as the young man tended his fields, the wife brought him a lunch. But once the evil sister came early and by the use of magic made him believe she was his wife. When the other arrived the two sisters fell to fighting, and the youth picked up a stone, but mistook the witch, and killed his own spouse. Thereupon the witch turned into a crow and flew away laughing.[6]

Old folk tales and myths such as this suggest that the Zuñi people held an abiding belief in witchcraft well before the coming of the Europeans. In 1539 a Spanish priest, Fray Marcos de Niza, commissioned by the viceroy of Mexico to explore the mysterious northland, entered the Zuñi country and viewed one of their pueblos (at that time there were six) from a distant mesa top. He approached no closer for he had already learned from servants that his chief guide, Estevanico, had been slain by the Indians. Estevanico, sometimes called Stephen the Black, was a Negro who had accompanied Cabeza de Vaca across the heartland of the Southwest during the years 1527-1536, thereby gaining valuable knowledge of native languages and ways. His appointment as Fray Marcos' scout had flattered his ego and he outfitted himself in grand style: bright cloth, hawks bells on his arms and legs, an Indian gourd rattle in his hand and a pack of greyhounds as his personal retinue. When the dark apparition appeared in Zuñi Pueblo, the Indians were astounded. This first man of the Old World they had ever seen told them by signs of his supernatural powers and asserted boldly that he was a powerful medicine man who could perform magical cures. If the Zuñis were as firmly wedded to belief in witchcraft at this early date as they were later in their history, it is safe to assume the village chiefs wasted little time in discussion before pronouncing the newcomer a member of the spellbinding tribe. In any event he was imprisoned in an adobe house outside the village, without food or water, and on the following day he was killed attempting to escape. His body was cut into small pieces and distributed to the headmen as proof that the victim had been mortal and not a god.[7] This was also an effective way to disperse the power of a witch.

During the three centuries of the Spanish colonial period occasional reports seeped out of the pueblo concerning witch scares or the entrapment of some luckless individual accused of practicing the black arts. Of more substance was a matter that came to the attention of the Spanish governor at Santa Fe in the year 1803. According to information supplied him by the alcalde mayor, that is, the chief magistrate who held jurisdiction over Zuñi, the pueblo council had met and decreed the death penalty for two witches of the village, a man and a woman, because they had brought excessive rains causing flooding of the crops. Before the harsh sentence could be carried out, the witchman had managed to flee with his family to the Pueblo of Acoma, but the woman was taken and sorely mistreated in an effort to force her to stop the rains. Investigation revealed that the male offender showed a long history of involvement with witchery and that his father had dealt in similar mysteries and had suffered public censure and punishment. Assessing the case, the Santa Fe governor, himself no scoffer in the efficacy of witchcraft, decreed that the escaped witch and his family be denied refuge in Acoma and that the accused take up residence in some pueblo near the capital so the Spanish authorities might keep watch over his activities.[8]

Not until the end of the nineteenth century when investigators such as Cushing, Stevenson, and others began a close study of Zuñi culture did the pueblo's obsession with witchcraft become apparent. It is difficult to judge whether the many serious instances of witchery reported at this time represented a sudden flare-up of witch mania or whether beneath the placid appearance of village life the fires of suspicion had always blazed with the same intensity. In either case it is certain that thoughts and dread of witchcraft were never far from the mind of a Zuñi.

Here, as at Nambé and elsewhere among the Pueblos, convicted witches, if it could be shown they had seriously injured or killed their victim, were sentenced to death. In those instances where a patient was cured by the medicine man usually through extraction of foreign matter "shot" into the body, the witch might be left unmolested, although there was sure to be much whispering against him. If the matter came to trial, the medicine man often testified that the accused's power was too strong and the patient had died, thus accounting for failure of the treatment.

Until prohibited by United States government authorities toward the end of the 1800s, public torture and execution of witches was an accepted feature of Zuñi life. The usual method was to draw the witch's arms back as far as possible and suspend him by the elbows from a projecting roof beam

in the ruins of the Spanish mission located in the center of
the pueblo. This place afforded all the populace a convenient
view of the victim's disgrace and last agony, but it also might
have been selected because some belief lingered that Christianity was a useful antidote in combating witchcraft. The
Zuñis had rejected Catholicism in the early nineteenth century and returned to their traditional religious practices, yet
a number of ideas picked up from the missionaries, particularly those related to witches, seem to have been adapted to
their own notions of supernaturalism. At Zuñi ashes are
rubbed on a baby to protect it from witches, a custom that
doubtless derived from the Catholic practice of marking a
cross on the forehead on Ash Wednesday. As a rule hanging
by the elbows brought about death within a few hours, but
if the unfortunate individual failed to expire within the
proper length of time, a member of the Bow Priesthood
struck him on the head with a war club, bringing matters
to a close and ending prolonged suffering.

From time to time other forms of punishment were dealt
to witches including beatings and wrenching of the thumbs.
In one episode a Zuñi sorcerer known to be responsible for
numerous crimes was discovered lurking at night near a ceremonial house while medicine men were performing a cure.
A guard captured him and offered to put an arrow through
him at once, but a medicine man insisted that he should execute the witch, as his power would cause the wounds to fester
and the flesh to rot before death. Yet when he fired the arrow,
the witch pulled it out of his back and arrogantly threw it at
the medicine man. Within a few weeks, however, the culprit
became ill and his flesh began to decay giving his house such
an odor that no one was left unconvinced regarding his
identity as a witch. When he died his funeral went unat-
tended except by the four or five men assigned to bury him.[9]

One purpose of the torture administered prior to execution
was to wring a confession from the suspect. This was particularly important if the witch was charged with causing a
drought or bringing an excessive amount of rain since these

irregular weather conditions threatened the pueblo's food supply. By learning the nature and the source of the spell that had produced the disastrous condition, the priesthood was better able to take countermeasures and restore the proper relationship with the elements. Any person caught handling owl or crow feathers in an unusual manner became a target for persecution because these birds were thought to frighten away other birds and hence keep away the rain.[10]

In a few cases the witch's act of confession was interpreted as vitiating his power and at the discretion of the Bow Priests he might be released.[11] The purpose of execution seems to have been primarily that of removing a harmful agent from society, with punishment a secondary consideration. Seldom were an accused's pleas or denials of guilt given any attention, for by the time he was brought to trial public opinion had already solidly condemned him for suspected or imagined witchcraft pursuits.

Some of our earliest descriptions of Zuñi witch trials come from Frank Cushing, who had access to the innermost precincts of community life. One time he returned to the village after an extended absence to discover his friends in the midst of a catastrophe — a searing windstorm persisted day after day choking up the springs, drying out the fields and river, and spreading dunes of sand over the surrounding valley. With destruction of the crops, the pueblo faced starvation, and debate raged in the council concerning the possible reason for the gods thus punishing their children. Inevitably the cause of the calamity was fastened upon a witch, in this case a hapless fellow named Big Belly.

In a trial lasting a day and a half, he was subjected to intensive interrogation, but for once the priesthood was unable to take decisive action. Cushing was summoned, given a prominent place in the council, and, owing to his "knowledge of the world," was requested to render an opinion. Since a man's life was at stake, the anthropologist entered a strong plea for clemency and urged that Big Belly be let off after making a sacrifice of shell and turquoise to halt the winds.

The Bow Priests acceded to this, but added a rather mild penalty of exile, and the accused escaped with his life.

Unluckily, however, the winds did not cease and another scapegoat had to be discovered. The issue became more imperative with the unexplained death of a beautiful girl who had been universally revered. Suspicion finally settled upon the maiden's uncle, an old man known as the Bat, and he was dragged in the night to a secret chamber and placed on trial for poisoning his niece and tampering with the weather.

Perhaps because his moderate views toward witches were now well known, Cushing was not invited to attend this court. The first he knew of the matter was when several men rushed past his door shouting, "A wizard! A wizard!" and the pueblo was thrown into bedlam. By this time the offender had been condemned and carried outside where his arms were pulled behind him and he was strung up with a rawhide rope. Four of the priests approached the moaning victim, berating and haranguing him, until dawn.

Cushing found himself in a delicate position, but buckling on a pistol he marched to the site, determined to intervene and save the Bat. To the Bow Priests engaged in the grisly work, he said, "I come with words. You may try the old man, but you must not kill him. The Americans will see you, or find it out, and tell their people who will say, 'The Zuñis murdered one of their own grandfathers.' That will bring trouble on you all."

But this speech was paid little heed, and the Bat was yanked higher from the ground while he groaned in a weak voice, "I die. I am dying." At last though, under the strain and agony, he agreed to confess, and the head priest ordered his body lowered. Gasping for breath, the Bat acknowledged that the charges were true, he had committed evil. "My father taught me fifty years ago, in the mountains of the summer snows. It was medicine that I used. You will find a bundle of it over the rafters in my highest room."

Immediately one of the attendants was sent, and he returned with a small bunch of twigs. This the old man identified as the source of his power, and he promised the rains would come in four days if he was released. When cut loose he staggered through the hostile crowd and sought his home. Yet by the fifth day no rains had descended and people whispered that the Bat had vowed vengeance on the entire priesthood. Shortly afterward he disappeared without a trace, silently executed and buried by his oppressors, and almost at once the dust storms were calmed and a deluge of rain watered the plain and the pueblo fields. The death of the Bat had broken the curse upon Zuñi.[12]

The strong-willed Matilda Stevenson, carrying out research at the pueblo a decade after Cushing, also had to contend with witch trials and executions. One midnight a friend knocked at her door and informed her that a member of the Sword Swallower fraternity, one of the most important in the village, had been found guilty of a witch murder and would be executed on the following day. Mrs. Stevenson learned that a patient being tended by the head Bow Priest had accused the man of bewitching him before he died, and the Sword Swallower had been taken before the judges and pressed to reveal details of his evil practice. The frightened fellow at first declared that he knew nothing of witchcraft, but then seeing that his guilt was already accepted, he confessed to injuring the deceased by touching his throat with his finger tips. The death penalty was assigned and the man was allowed to return home to spend the last few hours before dawn with his family.

Mrs. Stevenson threw on her clothes and hurried forth to find the Bow Priest, Naiuchi, and urge him to withdraw his verdict on grounds that he might be mistaken. The aged priest, however, was obdurate, even when warned that the Indian Agent would learn about the killing and send for soldiers to arrest him.

To Mrs. Stevenson he affirmed, "I shall hang this wizard, even though I displease you. I shall hang him though the United States Government put me in prison for one month, six months, a year, forever. He has killed my patient, and he must die." At this speech, the anthropologist recorded in her journal, "The light fell upon Naiuchi's face and the expression, usually so kind, was now set and stern. There was nothing of rage expressed, only the firm determination of a man bent upon doing his duty though he lost his life by the act."

Hastening to the home of the condemned man, she found him in a pathetic state. He sat on the floor leaning against the wall, resigned and calm, but, nonetheless, a picture of despair. His ill wife and pregnant daughter clung to him weeping. Taking his hand, Mrs. Stevenson said with emotion, "Have faith in me; I will save you." But the man, smiling faintly, replied, "No mother. You wish to save me, but you cannot. Naiuchi has spoken."

Her fortitude and her knowledge of Zuñi's ways of thought now came to Mrs. Stevenson's aid. She convened a court of her own, assembling the Bow Priests, and addressing them in terms they readily understood. Claiming to possess certain supernatural capabilities, she dauntlessly announced that having visited the accused in his house, she had deprived him of his power of sorcery and he was now harmless. The priests accepted this statement without question and forthwith raised their sentence of death.

Some time afterward an equally serious situation arose and the anthropologist was again drawn into a grim web of witchcraft proceedings. She was summoned to the council house and there discovered a young girl of twelve lying on a pallet and suffering from a severe case of hysteria. Her limbs twitched and jerked violently as her parents and brother attempted to restrain her. On the opposite side of the room sat a handsome youth of seventeen heavily guarded and charged with bewitching the afflicted maiden.

A theurgist was at work trying to relieve the case of hysteria and he had spread about the patient a line of sacred corn meal. Prayers came to his lips and as he implored the aid of the gods, he dropped medicine and fetishes into six gourds of water. After consecrating the water, he dipped ashes from the fireplace with eagle plumes and scattered them to the four directions for physical purification. The girl's body was rubbed with medicine water, following which the theurgist placed his lips on her breast and pretended to draw an object from her heart. This was deposited on the floor, covered with meal, then collected in a corn husk and carried from the room. Upon conclusion of the treatment, the trial began.

With great difficulty the invalid was induced to speak, relating in a shaky voice these details. "I was playing near my house," she said, "when this boy came to me and told me to go with him. I refused so he grabbed my hand, and as soon as he touched me I began to tremble and ran home." Her parents added, "In a short time our child was crazy, as you see her now."

The Bow Priests encircled the prisoner and demanded that he reveal the nature of the charm he had used to produce the spasms in the girl. But he remained silent in spite of dire threats of punishment, and for half an hour kept his head bowed as the questions assailed him. Finally, though, he spoke in low and careful words, giving an account of the circumstances that led to his acquisition of the powers of witchery.

According to his testimony, he had visited Santo Domingo Pueblo on the Rio Grande and with a companion of that village accosted the head of the Galaxy fraternity expressing a desire to learn the secrets of witchcraft. The elder man took the two boys to an inner room of his house at midnight and asked them for what purpose they wished to acquire arcane medicine. Both replied that they wanted a love charm to captivate girls. The headman instructed the pair in the use of a mysterious root medicine, directing them to bite off a small quantity, chew and spit it into their hands, and rub their palms together before shaking hands with the girl they wished to control. He also gave them another root to counteract the effect of the evil plant. The boy then related that he and his friend appeared in the streets of Santo Domingo on the following day and waylaid two maidens bearing water jars on their heads. They shook hands and as the girls set down the containers, their hearts began to fly around. Suddenly each of them began to jump and spin like a top, then they would pause and sleep a moment, only to resume a few seconds later their wild motions. "They hopped and ran about the streets," the Zuñi youth continued. "We did not make these girls our wives. They were too crazy. In a short time they died."

As he finished his story the audience sat staring at him entranced. Mrs. Stevenson noted the cleverness of the boy in weaving into his grotesque fabrication mention of an antidote, a good root to nullify the bad. The Bow Priests had not missed this point either and after some reflection they demanded that he produce his medicine. Accompanied by a guard he went to his house and returned shortly with his pockets stuffed with two kinds of roots. Stripping down to his beads, breechcloth, and moccasins, the youth scattered sacred corn meal on the floor around him and then chewed up a bite of the evil root. After spitting the juice on his hands and rubbing himself, he began to whirl and thrash about as if insane. Whenever he approached the girl on the pallet, she shook with new spasms and began to scream, while the parents attempted to restrain her flailing members. Altogether it was an unnerving spectacle and an appalling manifestation of wizardry.

When the boy had stretched the credulity of the judges to the limit, he chewed some of the good root and immediately regained his senses. Going to the patient's side, he placed his lips upon hers and pretended to draw out a foreign object, which he deposited in the corn meal. Next he obliged her to swallow three bits of the beneficial root. By this point the poor girl's hysteria had so increased that Mrs. Stevenson intervened and asked that the proceedings be temporarily halted.

During the night the witchboy managed to escape and flee the pueblo, but after some hard riding the guards recaptured him and brought him back to face a second trial. The chief

Bow Priest now challenged the veracity of the earlier tale. "You lie," he thundered. "You did not get your knowledge of witchcraft from Santo Domingo, and I am here to see that you speak the truth."

Realizing that his first recital was discredited, the boy began a new series of inventions. "Yes, I lied. I lied because I love my father and mother and sister and did not wish to speak of them. They are witches. I belong to the family of original witches. All my grandfathers were wizards. I have the plume offerings brought to this world by my witch ancestors. Jumping through a hoop of yucca empowers us to make ourselves into dogs, cats, coyotes, hawks, crows, and owls, so that we pass quickly and unknown about the country. We gather in an inner room of my mother's house where four ancient lamps hang, one on each wall, and by this light we sit and talk and make the rain-makers angry, so that they will not work. I can assume the form of a cat and pass through the smallest hole to enter a house. I can fill my mouth with cactus needles and shoot them through windows and destroy life. I have killed two infants, three girls, and two boys. Ancient prayer plumes are the source of my power."

This revelation threw the council into an uproar. The first thought was to seize the prayer plumes which the boy claimed were hidden in the mud walls of his mother's house. The mother fortunately was absent at one of the outlying farming communities, but a delegation entered her home with axes and commenced to hack away at the adobe plaster. Several bundles of feathers were actually discovered, confirming the boy's confession and practically sealing his fate. Again Mrs. Stevenson found herself in an uncomfortable position, determined to prevent a hanging, but wary lest she alienate her hosts and cause her research to be suspended. Also she could not be sure that her previous stratagem would work a second time.

With the Bow Priests' permission she was allowed a private talk with the youth, whose fantastic stories had so disturbed the Pueblo. She emerged from this conference to announce that the accused had been deprived of his diabolical arts, he could never practice them again, and hence he should not be hung. Once more the priesthood was moved by her plea, but a public confession and retraction were deemed necessary to assure the populace that it had nothing more to fear from this particular witch.

At the call of the Bow Priests everyone crowded into the plaza toward sunset. The confiscated medicine plumes were arrayed on the ground so that nobody would be denied an opportunity to gaze at these mysteries. The unfortunate boy, already exhausted by his ordeal, was kept talking far into the night, confessing anew his list of crimes and summarizing a life dedicated to witchcraft. In conclusion he proclaimed, "I did possess all the power of my wizard forefathers. It came to me through many generations. I have been all-powerful in witchcraft. But since visiting with my mother [Mrs. Stevenson] I have lost all my power. While with my mother, and while she talked to me, I felt my eyes change from black to blue, and then turn from blue to black, and then I felt that all my power of witchcraft was gone, not only for a little while, but for all time."

At these words the eager throng shouted, "Good! Good! Thanks, mother! Thanks!" And the head Bow Priest grasped the anthropologist's hand, expressing his gratitude and that of the people of Zuñi for robbing a witch of his power to destroy. Had Mrs. Stevenson remained permanently at the pueblo, the persecution of witches might have slowly subsided and then died out altogether.[13]

A serious case arose in 1894 involving a young man named Zuñi Nick. This individual had been raised in the home of a white Indian- trader, been away to school, and acquired a reputation as a free thinker and a scoffer of native religion and superstition. When a scourge of smallpox attacked the village and a fierce wind blew all the peaches off the fruit trees, Nick was convicted of causing these misfortunes and condemned to death. Hung by his thumbs from the beam of the old church, he yelled so loudly that his cries reached the

ears of his benefactor, the Indian trader, who came running
to the rescue waving a revolver. Thus providentially saved
from an agonizing death, Nick fled the pueblo and went to
nearby Fort Wingate where he entered charges against the
Zuñi governor and other officials for failing to protect him.
These persons, though having no real part in the affair, were
arrested by the soldiers and held in confinement for several
months.[14]

When Matilda Stevenson left Zuñi, Naiuchi of the Bow
Priesthood gave her a set of prayer plumes and sacred medicine, used to identify evildoers, asking that she show them
to the President as conclusive proof that witches did exist
in the pueblo. Concern was growing among the Indians that
increasing government interference would hinder the pursuit and elimination of witches, placing the entire community in peril. For them the white man's disbelief in witchcraft
was unfathomable, and resentment flared that in so important a matter outsiders presumed to meddle in the personal
concerns of the pueblo.[15]

George Wharton James, a tourist and popular writer on
the Southwest who visited Zuñi several years after the departure of Cushing and Stevenson, had occasion to witness both
the tragic persecution of a witch and the confrontation between the Indian way and the white man's law. Arriving in
the village one afternoon, he learned that an ancient crone
named Melita was at that moment hanging from the church
by her thumbs, condemned for practicing witchcraft. As
James wrote later, "The poor old wretch, friendless and for-
lorn, had been accused of causing the death of Wé-wha, one
of the most noted women of the tribe."

Certain that the visitor would try to intercede on behalf
of their witch, the priests unstrung her and hurried her off
to a secluded apartment out of sight. James confronted
Naiuchi and demanded to know what had become of the
victim, but his question was met with stony silence. In a
state of righteous indignation, he began a search of the village and after several hours discovered Melita, "sick almost

to death as the result of the cruel treatment she had received. Her wrists were cut through to the bone, her back all lacerated with the beatings she had received, and her cheeks even were broken where the blood had burst through the veins." At James's request several government teachers cared for the poor woman's wounds and provided her food while troops were summoned from Fort Wingate. The soldiers arrested Naiuchi and accomplices and conveyed them to jail in Albuquerque to await trial.[16] The day when the Zuñis could publicly execute delinquents on witch charges had come to an end.

Although the Indians by necessity moderated their treatment of persons convicted of witchcraft, a preoccupation with supernatural phenomena has given no sign of abating in the twentieth century. Persons even today scrupulously avoid walking about late at night lest their motives be placed in question, and home owners keep curtains drawn after sundown so that wizards and witches may not peep into the family circle and cause harm. Anthropologist Florence Hawley reports that one of her students after World War II was a young Zuñi veteran who chose to attend The University of New Mexico on the GI Bill rather than return to his pueblo where, as previous experience showed, he was subject to constant illness caused by witches. His only alternative if he remained at home was to join one of the curing societies, a procedure involving a lengthy initiation, periodic religious retreats, and other heavy obligations. By escaping to the white man's world, he was freed from the clutches of witches and the onerous burden of membership in a curing society.[17]

For several years during the 1940s an unusual number of Zuñis died from a malady the Indians described in this way: "Your blood turns to water and when this happens it comes out your mouth mixed with white spots and you are gone. It takes a long time for some people to die. If they aren't strong they die right away. Others live for a few months and then their bowels get bad and they begin spitting out blood which turns to water. Nothing can help them."

The popular view held that the origin of this infirmity lay with witches who had buried bad medicine at several points around the village, for whenever some hapless person stepped on one of these spots he caught the disease and died. Finally a woman came screaming from her house late at night claiming that a thirteen-year-old boy had tried to molest her. The lad was discovered hiding naked in a corral and was dragged before a meeting of Bow Priests. Under cross-examination he began to cry and confessed having a part in the witch-caused epidemic. He declared that he was weary of killing people and had assaulted the woman, knowing that he would be caught and brought to justice. Among other crimes, he claimed to have killed his stepfather and stepmother because he was angry with them and to have brought sickness upon six or seven people who had died during the year. He further incriminated his whole party of witches: "They killed most of the people who have died of this sickness. There is medicine buried in almost all of the pueblo."

The boy's clothes were found and brought before the court. A Bow Priest drew two soft-boiled eggs from the pockets, one decorated with lightning designs and the other with strange blue and green crosses. A curious wad of rags accompanied the eggs. The young witch explained that he had planned to bury these things in the ground where the women sit at stone mealing bins to grind corn. As the eggs rotted, the evil would come up out of the ground, enter their bodies, and infect them with the fatal illness that had been sweeping the village. Carried away by his own words, the boy expanded "Now I am glad you know all this. I don't want to go on doing this witch work. There are lots of us in Zuñi. That is what is causing all this disease. There is medicine buried in lots of the houses. One medicine is buried by a road leading into the village. Another is on the trail across the river; several people have stepped over it and died."

Following this disclosure, the people raised a clamor demanding that the rascal be hung, but the head priest, mind-

PLATE 6. *Zuñi Pueblo, site of several notorious witch-trials.*
(Ben Wittick photograph, Museum of New Mexico)

ful of the prison terms suffered by predecessors, announced, "No, if we hang him, the Agent would find it out and send us to the penitentiary. It is the white man's fault all these people are being killed. In the old days we could have hung these witches and stopped this disease. Now we can do nothing." Some solace was found in blaming the white man, and the Indians went out grumbling that they were both misunderstood and deemed crazy because they attempted to protect themselves from the evils of witchcraft. The Agent, when he learned of the affair, quickly got the accused boy out of the village and sent him away to school.[18]

With executions now in abeyance at Zuñi, the Bow Priests are reduced to giving witch suspects a serious "talking to." This may entail hours of nagging questions and accusations and the defendant usually confesses something so that he can bring the ordeal to a conclusion. Although alleged witches need not fear corporal punishment, their position in the pueblo after a trial can be made so uncomfortable they often find it convenient to move either to one of the satellite farming communities or to the city of Gallup, thirty miles to the north.

From witch cases and trials depicted by early observers, several interesting practices and customs may be noted. The Zuñis believed that catching a witch was easier if you turned all your clothes inside out, a method that clearly derived from neighboring Hispanos. To join a society, or "witch party" as the boy in the aforementioned story called it, a candidate was required to bewitch someone to death, ordinarily a member of his own household. To obtain aid in planting a hex, a witch might act through the ghosts of departed relatives of his victim. Since those engaged in sorcery make use of hair cuttings, the Zuñis burn or throw into the river all clippings from the head.[19] Witches are able to fly by placing crow and owl feathers in their hair and flapping their arms, or by stepping into a dust devil (small wind funnel). Other characteristics of Zuñi belief are revealed in the following incidents.

Account by a Government Teacher, 1880

"One sad event of the year was a trial, and I have no doubt the death, of an old Indian, who by the other Indians was supposed to be a witch. The charges laid against him were, first: as is their custom, they plant plumes, but this old man was charged with having planted owl feathers, and such feathers are used only by witches. Another charge was that he had bewitched two young girls of the village, who afterwards died. By planting owl feathers, he caused all the high wind. This wind raised the sand which killed their corn by its blowing over the fields. At two o'clock in the night an alarm was raised in the town. At sunup next morning the witch was caught, his hands tied behind his back, and then tied up to a pole so that his feet barely touched the ground. While in this position, his life was threatened, and there and then (July 4, 1880) they made him confess to the charges laid against him. I understand these things were done by direction of the War Captain. I told Pedro Pino that if they killed him I would report the whole matter to the Agent, who was expected in Zuñi in a few days. Everything was quiet until Agent Thomas came and went; then one morning the old witch was reported dead and buried. An Indian told some Americans in town that they had killed him."[20]

Experience of a Badger Clan Member

"At one time I had a very bad throat, which was much swollen and very painful. The theurgist came and soon discovered the cause of my suffering. A witch had shot a stone into my throat. The theurgist had to repeat many prayers to the Blest Gods before power was given him to extract the stone. He had to place his hands upon my throat and call with great power, but obedient to his command, the foreign matter finally appeared. It was, he averred, a large, ugly stone, and he immediately cast it into the fire as unfit for my mother and me to see."[21]

A Flying Wizard

"A certain wizard painted his body red and the scalp-knot

white. He placed wreaths of yucca around his wrists and ankles, and then entered the whirlwind, which is the friend of witches, headforemost. He traveled to the great river of the west and returned to Zuñi in one day. He went to the great river to steal the plume-offerings deposited by the rain priests near Zuñi and carried by the butterflies attached to the plume-sticks to the great river.

"The whirlwind, becoming weary, dropped the wizard a short distance from Zuñi, and as he fell, a youth passing by exclaimed: 'Aha, where have you been? Man, you are a sorcerer or you would not be traveling in the whirlwind.' The youth followed the wizard to the village and told his story, and it was discovered that the man was a wizard and had stolen the plume-offerings of the rain priests. The wizard belonged to the Dogwood Clan. He was tried by the Bow Priesthood and was convicted and hung by the arms. No food was given him, and at the end of one night and a day he died."[22]

8

Montezuma, a Sacred Snake, and Pecos Pueblo

ACCORDING TO A POPULAR New Mexican folk myth, Montezuma was born among the Rio Grande Indians and in his youth moved to the old Pueblo of Pecos where he became recognized as a great ruler and assumed the role of cacique or head priest. Because of his wise leadership the Pecos people grew in prosperity and numbers, and members of other, less fortunate villages asked to join them and share in the bounty. Montezuma possessed vast supernatural power enabling him to control the elements, to guarantee good hunting for his people, and to predict future events. When he was ready to take a bride, he sent an emissary to request the hand of the youngest daughter of the cacique of Zuñi, and the entreaty was successful because the Zuñis wished to be allied with this powerful lord. Thus the girl Malinche traveled one hundred leagues across the Southwest desert to become the queen of Montezuma.

When at last Pecos became too crowded, Montezuma climbed aboard an eagle, and ordering some of the people to follow him, he took up a long journey to the south. Each place the eagle alighted, some of the Indians stopped and built a new pueblo, while the remainder of the multitude proceeded in the wake of their winged leader. After many days the bird seized a snake in its beak and settled upon a prickly pear cactus, and here Montezuma ordered the building of a great city, destined to become Tenochtitlán (Mexico City), the capital of his empire.[1]

Anglo-Americans who visited the far Southwest in the early nineteenth century invariably mentioned the Montezuma tale in their chronicles. The Pueblo Indians, they noted, referred to themselves as descendants of Montezuma, and they held special feasts and dances around a pole in honor of this mythic hero. Since many of these writers were familiar with the classic historical works of Humboldt and Prescott that referred to the migration of the Aztecs from some remote northern province, they assumed that the prevalence of the Montezuma legend along the Rio Grande meant that New Mexico was indeed the original homeland of the wandering tribe whose empire Cortes had toppled in Central Mexico. In any case it was clear that the Pueblos knew a great deal about an epic figure called Montezuma and that he appeared prominently in their mythology.

In an earlier chapter we have seen that the historical Montezuma, who ruled the Aztec Empire from 1503 until his death in 1520, was something of a mystic and a devotee of witchcraft. But as he appears in the folk literature of the southwestern Indians, he is usually represented as a culture hero closely allied with good spirits and dedicated to beneficent activities. Yet since even the best among Pueblo persons and gods possess a dual capacity for good and evil, the mythic history of Montezuma contains within it the suggestion that black as well as white magic were sources of power tapped by the legendary hero.

Fray Alonso de Benavides, that seventeenth century friar haunted by the notion of a Pueblo population divided solely into warrior and sorcerer classes, recorded in 1634 his own version of the Aztec migration out of New Mexico. According to him, the Indians of the Southwest had once been one people but through connivance of the Devil they split into two warring factions. Satan himself led one group south to the spot where an eagle perched on a prickly pear, and here was laid the foundations of the Aztec State. The other faction, called Taos, remained in the north and were the progenitors of all the Pueblo Indians later encountered by the Spaniards.

These were directed by another demon, an old woman in the guise of a witch, tall and thin; possessing a large mouth filled with fangs; sagging, flabby breasts; claws on her hands, feet, and heels; and a head covered with coarse, gray, matted hair. Once the Aztecs had departed, the witch placed an enormous boulder of iron on her head and informed the Taos that with this object she would mark the southern boundary of their country, in present Chihuahua, and they must never venture beyond it.

Fray Alonso relates:

> The boulder can be seen by everyone today. I have personally seen it several times. Stamped upon it are the marks of the infernal old woman's claws, feet, and hands, as well as the nails of her hands with which she appeared to have kneaded it as if it were of wax. Her very head with its tangled hair, upon which she had borne the globe, is there stamped. In the judgment of all those who see it, it is believed to weigh more than two hundred quintals, while others think that it weighs more. It is as wide as the largest wagon wheel and must be almost eight spans high. All those who travel back and forth from New Mexico see it. The horses used to shy at it and would not approach nearby, but one of our friars a few years ago exorcised it and said Mass over it, so that the horses lost their fear and today approach it without recoiling, even climbing over it.[2]

A contemporary of Benavides, Fray Gerónimo de Zárate Salmerón, also saw the witch stone and made reference to it.

> It is an ancient tradition among the Indians that a piece of virgin iron which is three leagues from Santa Bárbara, half a league away from the road over which the carts that go to New Mexico pass, is a memorial to the coming of the Aztecs to settle this land. . . . They say that a demon in the form of an old Indian woman who was very wrinkled brought it on her back. Some feat for an old Indian woman![3]

Scholars have long speculated upon the way Montezuma entered Pueblo folklore and oral literature. It is now generally conceded that the Spaniards and their Mexican-Indian servants spread the story of the conquest of the Aztecs and their emperor among the Rio Grande Indians, and that within a short time Montezuma became fully incorporated into Pueblo mythology. Often he was associated with Pohé-yemo, the culture hero of ancient tradition, who reputedly worked the magic that led to the sucessful Indian revolt of 1680. Sometimes the two are identified as the same being, but on occasion Pohé-yemo appears as Montezuma's lieutenant.[4] In any event Montezuma, the producer of powerful wonders through supernatural means, was a revered figure in the Pueblo pantheon and came to symbolize the underlying core of Indian unity standing in opposition to innovations brought first by the Spaniards and later by Anglo-Americans.

The Montezuma legend was present among practically all southwestern Indian groups, although the details of his activity vary widely. Most tribes credit Pecos with being the seat of Montezuma's operations prior to his eagle flight southward, but in some variants of the tale Taos Pueblo figures more prominently. A hunting party of Santo Domingo Indians told Lt. A. W. Whipple in the early 1850s that Montezuma had been born at a place called Acoti and that he taught the Indians how to build multi-storied adobe pueblos and underground kivas for their ceremonies. Taos had been the first village he founded and from there he moved south establishing settlements and instructing the people.[5]

The Taos Indians themselves held that the summit of the tallest mountain behind their pueblo was the spot where Montezuma had promised to make a reappearance among his chosen people. Some of the villagers once followed a reckless young Spaniard part way up the mountain and halted as he went on alone to scale the last peak. From the top he shouted back that he had found a great cavern filled with the gold of Montezuma's treasure, but at that moment he was caught up by a whirlwind and a bolt of lightning split the trail apart. The terrified Indians fled down the slope leaving the fool-hardy Spaniard to his fate and the supernatural powers in possession of the gold.[6]

Pecos, situated near the headwaters of the Pecos River some twenty miles east of Santa Fe, was the largest of all of the pueblos when the Spaniards first reached the Southwest in 1540. Its numbers steadily dwindled during the three succeeding centuries owing mainly to inroads of smallpox and raids by hostile Comanches. By 1838 a wretched handful of survivors abandoned the village and sought refuge at kindred-speaking Jémez Pueblo beyond the Rio Grande. The tragic end of Pecos left a strong impression upon the minds of other Pueblo people who ascribed its decline to supernatural causes rather than to disease and warfare.

Many Indians believed that Montezuma, before his departure for Mexico centuries before, had kindled a sacred fire and entrusted its maintenance to the Pecos, enjoining them to keep the blaze alive until he returned to deliver his people from the yoke of the Spaniards. Josiah Gregg, a Santa Fe trader who paused briefly at the pueblo in the early 1830s, claimed to have descended into one of the kivas and "beheld this consecrated fire, silently smoldering under a covering of ashes, in the basin of a small altar."[7] Other accounts, particularly those of native informants, contend that the fire was kept in a cave, the mouth of which was visible from the doorway of the mission church. Somehow, popular tradition ran, the guardians of the blaze neglected their duty, allowing the fire to die out, and this was the real reason the town had to be abandoned. In one rendering twelve virgin daughters of the village's head men had been given charge of supplying firewood, but becoming drowsy one winter night they fell asleep and permitted the holy flame to perish and the altar to grow cold.[8]

Gregg, on the contrary, says that tending of the fire was allotted to a group of warriors who kept watch by turns for two successive days and nights, without partaking of either food, water, or sleep. The severity of this schedule produced exhaustion and even death among the keepers until none was left to carry on the sacred duty.[9] Lt. James W. Abert, in reporting still another version, declared that a single Indian maintained a vigil over the fire for the space of a year, and he always died in the ensuing year, worn out by his labors. "This custom caused the extinction of the tribe," he says.[10]

The legend of the Pecos fire receives further embellishment with mention of a giant snake god to whom was fed infants and the bodies of those dying from overwork in the performance of ceremonial functions. Josiah Gregg wrote that "on one occasion I heard an honest ranchero assert, that entering Pecos very early on a winter's morning, he saw the huge trail of the reptile in the snow, as large as that of an ox being dragged."[11] Abert adds that Pecos had "the custom of offering infant children, to appease the wrath of an evil spirit, to a serpent which some represent as an idol, others as a serpent of real existence."[12]

Throughout Puebloland, on pottery, cave and kiva walls, and even on dance kilts, may be found decorations representing a feathered or horned snake. Without doubt this ancient motif traces its origin to the central Mexican plumed serpent which was one of the manifestations of the Aztecs Quetzalcoatl, the God of Learning and the Priesthood. At the Pecos ruins archaeologists have discovered long tubular pipes of clay ornamented in relief with horned snakes to whom were attributed the life-giving rains of summer.[13] Precisely when the Pueblos first linked Montezuma, the sacred fire, and a snake god to Pecos is not certain, but that they did connect them to the mythological history of this village cannot be disputed.

A story concerning the Pecos snake deity collected from a San Ildefonso Indian in 1930 illustrates the strength and persistence of the old legend. The Pecos people possessed a serpent god which they kept in a kiva and by whose favor they prospered in all things. In return for his patronage hunters went out each day to secure fresh meat as the snake had a voracious appetite. Once the men of the village became distracted with other things and failed to provide food, and when the god called for his meal they paid no attention. Finally the snake became angry and decided to leave his subjects to their own devices. When the kiva guardians were all asleep, he slithered out the hatchway and disappeared to the west leaving a track as deep as a small arroyo.

A few days later several San Ildefonsos were hunting along the Galisteo River when they were surprised to see two Pecos Indians, clad only in loincloths as when hunting, running toward them in a very excited state. Some of the hunters advanced to learn what was the matter and the Pecos asked them if they had seen their snake god. When the San Ildefonsos said they had seen nothing, the two replied, "It is well that you did not, for he might have bitten you. We have tracked him this far, but we cannot find him." Continuing on the trail as far as Santo Domingo, the Pecos observed where their serpent had disappeared into the Rio Grande, and with this they gave up hope and returned home. The loss so dispirited the few remaining residents of the pueblo that they deserted their houses and went to reside with relatives in Jémez.[14]

Hispanos living in the vicinity of Taos Pueblo once believed the Indians of that village harbored a divine snake. Cleo Jaramillo, who recorded many folk traditions of northern New Mexico, mentioned that the Taos had a rich gold mine in the mountains and a *biborón* ("monster rattlesnake") to which they fed infants on special feast days. Early in 1847, when American military forces assailed Mexican and Indian rebels forted up in the pueblo, the great serpent was endangered, so he was moved to safety across the river in a handcart covered with blankets. The man who braved the fire was shot to pieces, but not before he dropped the *biborón* into a kiva where it was preserved. Some tale tellers contend that it was a live reptile, while others say it was a mere idol.[15]

It appears that Montezuma, the sacred fire that was to be kept burning in his honor, the giant snake that ate infants, and deceased fire-keepers all became fused in popular myth.

The supernatural attributes of Montezuma and the favors he bestowed upon the Pueblo people gave him the status of a culture hero. When the Spaniards threatened the Indians with cannon, according to native history Montezuma intervened and declared he would bring forth a larger gun to oppose the aggressors. To prove the power of their weapons, the Spaniards blew a hole through a tree with a single cannon ball. But the Indian lord called down thunder from the clouds and split the tree from top to bottom.

In his role as a mythic deity Montezuma emerged as the protector of native religion and many of the feats ascribed to him, such as the ability to plant a kernel of corn one night and harvest mature ears on the following morning, were similar to those said to be performed by the Indian priesthood in their kivas. The Spanish clergy, in denouncing all practices of the medicine men as sorcery and proclaiming the Indian gods agents of the Devil, inadvertently augmented the prestige of Montezuma among the Pueblos. To the Indian mind Motezuma's resort to arcane powers, the same powers misused by witches, was necessary to nullify the harm caused by Catholic and, later in the nineteenth century, by Protestant missionaries. Magic turned to positive purposes was one of the strongest weapons in the arsenal of Montezuma and the Indian caciques and priests, and only by its use was some semblance of the native religious system preserved.

9

Navajo and Apache Witchcraft

WEST OF THE RIO GRANDE and adjacent to the pueblos of
the Zuñi and Hopi live today better than one hundred thousand Navajos, forming the largest Indian tribe within the
United States. Their country, stretching hundreds of square
miles across northern New Mexico and Arizona, is a land of
arid, sage-studded wastes, awesome canyons, and rock-ribbed
mountains. Scattered in isolated encampments and living in
eight-sided, dome-roofed hogans, the Navajos eke out a precarious living tending flocks of sheep and goats; manufac-
turing silver and turquoise jewelry, and brilliant-hued blankets; and raising corn, vegetables, and fruit trees in an occasional pocket where rainfall collects or a spring overflows.

In complexity and richness of ceremonialism, Navajo religion rivals that of the neighboring Pueblos; and, indeed,
the Navajos during the past several centuries appear to have
borrowed, elaborated upon, and integrated into their own
ritual patterns many elements of supernaturalism belonging
to the village Indians. Since they were remote from the centers of Spanish settlement in colonial times, the Navajos, unlike the Rio Grande Pueblos, were scarcely troubled by
Catholic friars, but after 1870 they began to experience the
inroads of American missionaries. Representatives of Protestant, Mormon, and Catholic groups built churches and
established missions in the farthest reaches of the reservation
and struggled with one another to attract the largest membership among the Indians.

Although the missionaries have been in Navajoland for a hundred years and their denominations today number more than thirty, their work can scarcely be rated a success. The fact is, many aspects of Christianity directly contradict Navajo religious beliefs and taboos, and some white ministers have been known to remark sadly, after a lifetime of labor, that they know not a single Indian who has fully understood or accepted Church doctrine.

Something that no amount of Christian teaching has ever been able to eradicate is the Navajos' fear of the dead and of ghosts, a dread that approaches a tribal phobia. In their belief, contact with the dead is the worst horror that can be imagined, and a great deal of all ceremonial procedure is directed toward exorcising evil resulting from accidental encounters with bodies of the departed. Elaborate taboos and ritual formulas are strictly observed by all individuals to neutralize the harmful effects produced by a chance confrontation with a ghost or witch or by stumbling upon a corpse. In this context it may be readily understood why the Navajos look with abhorrence upon a religion such as Christianity that presented its divine hero as a god risen from the dead. Far from giving them spiritual comfort, the white man's theology in singling out their main obsession, fear of the dead, infects the Navajos with profound anxiety and offers not a shred of solace.[1]

Ghosts and witches are closely associated in both Navajo religion and mythology, and as witches cause death through exercise of diabolic acts, they are regarded with special repugnance. In Navajo teaching, the deities First Man, First Woman, and Coyote receive responsibility for introducing witchcraft. Leaving the Underworld the unholy three passed through various levels of the universe before reaching earth, and at each stop along their journey they were forced to move on again after a short pause because their witchery made them so unpopular. In the Seventh World they found Cat People who themselves were witches, but First Man humbled them and arrogated their evil power to himself before continuing upward.[2] Reaching the surface of the world, the deities perceived the forbears of the Navajo living untutored and in confusion and strongly addicted to all forms of antisocial behavior. To them First Man and First Woman offered to provide stability and knowledge, but with an organized world the Indians also had to accept witchcraft, disease, and death. To offset these curses the Navajos obtained more than two dozen medicine "sings" or chants, one of the most potent being the Upward-reaching-way or "Witch Chant."[3] These incredibly long and elaborate ceremonials form the matrix of Navajo religious faith and serve as the rock from which efforts are launched to appease or oppose the unseen forces of the supernatural world.

The linking of Coyote to the travels of First Man and First Woman is significant, for he represents the arch-trickster and embodies numerous aspects of malign power. Over and over again he interferes detrimentally with the affairs of men and through his vast fund of evil knowledge produces havoc in human institutions. Often he does the bidding of First Woman, for all she has to do is will something bad to happen and Coyote carries out her wishes and makes people ill.[4]

Because the Coyote deity is so malevolently inspired — indeed in some accounts he is pictured as the sign and symbol of witchcraft — Navajos go to great pains to avoid his earthly progeny, the small, dust-colored animals that skulk about refuse heaps and yip at a full moon. If a Navajo starts an important journey and finds that his trail crosses the path of a coyote, he will dare not proceed for fear of bad luck, but instead returns home and waits three days before setting out anew. He believes that the Devil, a figure borrowed from the Whites, uses a coyote for his steed and lopes about on nightly errands. A Navajo who has led a wicked life may be transformed into a coyote at death, or alternately into an owl or crow. Since the Navajo language, notwithstanding its complexity, is deficient in contemptible words, the most insulting thing one may may call another is a coyote.[5]

In practically the same manner as European peasants of

the late Middle Ages, Navajos believe in were-animals, or witches who transform themselves into beasts so that they may move about at night with speed and greater freedom. To effect a metamorphosis, Navajo witches don the skin of a coyote, wolf, bear, or fox which is kept hanging in a cave when not needed. The guise of a werewolf, just as in the Old World, is most popular. Any Indian who comes upon a wolf with his tail hanging straight down will kill it, since to his way of thinking it has to be a witch. Real wolves, as he knows, always run holding the tail out behind. If he manages to shoot the animal in the heart, it will return home and change back into human form before dying.[6]

There are various sources of evil in the Navajo view of the cosmos, but the worst of these pertains to sorcery and witchcraft. This finds expression in a fear of persons, places, and objects that have become identified with the wizardly arts. Witches employ bad medicine and practice their trade in secret to kill other members of the tribe. As theirs is the most heinous crime, trials formerly resulted in a sentence of death. But today, under outside pressure, punishment is less severe.

Among the Navajo, men are more often practitioners of witchcraft than women. Invariably female witches are old and, according to some sources, childless.[7] Aged men, affected by senility, may become suspect, but generally care is lavished upon them to prevent the development of antagonism. Everyone tries discreetly to get rid of such persons by urging them to visit a distant family, which in turn will pass them on to others.[8]

Witches, in the performance of their craft, gather at night to plot against victims, initiate new members, enjoy intercourse with dead women, and practice cannibalism, activities that sound quite similar to those indulged in by traditional covens of European witches. On the floor of a cave where they convene, the witches may make a sand painting of ashes representing the person they intend to kill. With a magic bow they shoot the figure with beads, and these wing through the air seeking out the real victim and entering his body no

PLATE 7. *Navajo medicine men preparing a sand painting; these are used in ceremonies to cure natural and supernatural illnesses. (Museum of New Mexico photograph)*

matter how far away he may be. A variation of this technique, said to be relied upon by some Navajo sorcerers, is that of "bean shooting." In this method a witch man propels white beans into the air, and after four days' travel they strike the victim and cause his death. If the person so bedeviled discovers the source of his trouble in time, he may call in a medicine man who will make an incision and suck out the offending beans. This cure has to be undertaken with consummate speed, however, because any delay proves fatal. Occasionally when witches make an error in this ritual, the flying beans hunt fruitlessly for their prey and then return to wound mortally those who originally shot them out. Thus the concoction of magic can be a hazardous enterprise if adequate safeguards are neglected.[9]

When witches assemble in their murky caves, they sit in a circle, nude except for masks, and surrounded by baskets of human flesh. Chants, directed by a chief witch, help in conjuring up bad medicine, and the congregation periodically spits and urinates upon sand pictures. From the walls of the cave human heads or skulls gaze down with sightless eyes upon the phantasmal scene, macabre relics of the witches' past successes.[10]

Lightning is the most powerful weapon available to those dedicated to sorcery, but its unpredictable properties and its tendency to turn upon the user are so well known that few witches dare bring it into play. In the late 1930s seven Navajos were killed by lightning and the witch responsible for the tragedy was easily identified. Yet because of the immensity of the deed, showing the evil force at his command, he escaped retribution. No one felt sufficiently confident to challenge him with good medicine.

An ancient Navajo petroglyph, or rock drawing, discovered near Manuelito on the Arizona-New Mexico border, shows an owl figure being struck by lightning. Indian interpretation of this picture reveals that the owl represents a man who has been bewitched, and the lightning, springing from the four points of the compass, has sought out its victim and

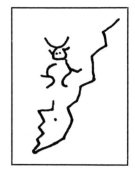

entered his body to kill him. Either a long-ago witch drew this emblem as an aid in working his lethal spell, or he placed it on the rock surface after the event to commemorate the success of his project.[11]

Careless handling not only of lightning but any form of black medicine may easily boomerang and turn against the witch who uses it. Once an important Navajo came under suspicion of sorcery because of a sudden rise in his material fortunes. The assumption seemed to be confirmed when he pawned a silver bracelet recognized as having been buried with a rich girl's corpse. Only a witch can rob a grave with impunity. Years later when the man became ill, he paid to have several curing chants sung over him, but they offered no relief and his condition grew worse. Consulting a native doctor noted for divination, he learned the illness was the result of his earlier robbing of the dead. Realizing his own sorcery had turned against him, the Navajo confessed, arranged for a new chant to void the evil he had set loose, and recovered. Those who learned of the episode whispered that the witch had not been able to manage his power and it had gotten out of control causing his misfortune.[12]

This case illustrates a common feature of Navajo witchcraft belief; that is, many persons are tempted to enter evil paths by a desire for wealth. Since witches have no fear of the dead, they may cause the death of rich people and then loot their graves of valuable blankets, jewelry, and beads. Another way to profit is through fee-splitting. The conjurer infects his victim with disease and subsequently sends his partner, an unscrupulous physician, to produce a cure at exorbitant cost, and the two divide the fee.[13]

While a sudden or unexepected display of wealth may cause someone to be pegged as a witch, an even more serious cause for suspicion is any form of incest. This aberration is intimately associated with all forms of witchcraft, unnatural father-daughter relations or sexual relations with a clan sister being those most frequently mentioned.

Until fairly recent times, a confirmed case of witchcraft more often than not brought summary execution. A Rio Grande newspaper in 1895 reported one such incident from western New Mexico. "A few days ago a foul murder was committed among the Navajos at or near the Hendricks' cow camp on the Chaco. An old Navajo man was accused of being a witch, as it is alleged by the Indians that he made their children sick every time he came around. When finally they captured him, one buck held him while the squaws stoned him to death. The old Navajo's sons are on the war path, and trouble is expected among the Indians, as several of them have been trying to borrow guns and ammunition."[14]

Because sorcery and witchery flourish and anyone may be victimized, Navajos devote much attention to providing themselves with protection. Presence of prayer sticks and similar ceremonial objects in the hogan offers some insurance, as does the strewing of salt around the encampment.[15] Even today many old-fashioned Navajos will carry "witch medicine" on their persons to ward off attack, especially when they are in a large crowd. Such medicine is most salutary when composed of corn meal mixed with the gall of an eagle, bear, mountain lion, or skunk.[16]

Any strong medicine, it is generally agreed, gives good defense against the barbed arrows of witches. Curers and ceremonial chanters, because of the power at their command, believe they are immune from spells and enchantment. Medicine men, since they have knowledge of the inner workings of witchcraft, are better able to protect themselves than average persons, but if they make use of occult practices too freely it may work to their detriment and taint their reputations.[17]

Disease, whether the result of "natural causes" or the work of a witch, is treated by an expensive curing ritual the aim of which is to cast out the evil. Traditional ceremonials are most effective against the old illnesses, and in fact many practitioners admit that their medicine will not cure maladies introduced by the white man. A few years ago a Navajo medicine man was accused of witchcraft because his step-son and several other youths in the neighborhood succumbed to tuberculosis. For this new and loathsome disease, which takes a heavy toll among the Indians, there is no native cure. The medicine man was brought to trial and might well have paid the supreme penalty had not a friendly trader rescued him and sent him to live on a distant part of the reservation where he was unknown.[18]

The experience of one Navajo man who fell ill attests to the problems that may arise even when accepted curing procedures are followed. This individual resided near Shiprock and aroused the jealousy of many people owing to his wealth in sheep, horses, and cattle. Somewhere among the envious was a witch who shot an object into his body producing an enormous abscess. The most famous native doctors were consulted and the man submitted to every "sing" known to the Navajo, but his condition failed to show any marked improvement. Next he sought out the services of a famous Hopi curer at the village of Oraibi. But in spite of prodigious efforts attended by much shouting, sweating, and writhing, this medicine man had no greater success in extracting the intrusive object. At last the patient was carried by his family to Santo Domingo Pueblo on the Rio Grande where a man dressed in a bearskin performed a strenuous cure and drew out "a piece of bone from some dead fellow." From that point on his health began to return, but the ordeal had so impoverished him that he never did recoup his former fortune.[19]

A tale dating from the mid-nineteenth century but still current among the Indians illustrates the way witch power may be summoned as an open and respected ally. A war party of Navajos had a camp on a mesa top from which they sallied forth periodically to sweep up flocks of Mexican sheep. One day they spied a company of militia following the stock trail and knew they would soon have a fight on their hands. The Mexicans stopped at the foot of the mesa to look over the country and several of the oldest Indians decided to try and kill their captain through wizardry. One man who was to do the "magic shooting" took out a red basket from a buckskin bag and placed it in his lap. He laid two blades of yucca across the basket with their sharp tips pointing at the enemy and in the bottom of the receptacle placed an olivella shell that had been rubbed with an eagle feather. As he chanted, the shell began to move, slowly at first and then faster. After the second song, it came shooting out of the basket like a bullet, and the Navajos had to duck their heads as it whistled past.

Shortly the Mexicans gave a yell and at once began to build a campfire. Several Indians who understood Spanish crept close and learned that the captain had suddenly gotten sick "from a red ant bite over the heart." His cries of pain could be clearly heard. In the morning the Mexicans began packing up and a Navajo, stealing into the camp again, heard that their leader had died toward daylight. This story is still related to Navajo young people as proof that some of their ancestors possessed exceptional power.[20]

South of the Navajos, in the White Mountains and adjacent ranges of eastern Arizona, dwell the Western Apaches, speaking the same language and sharing at least some beliefs in witchcraft and black magic. The Apaches, while not quite so timorous of the dead, have an abiding fear of shooting sorcerers, witch sickness, enchanted lightning, and, if it is malevolently inspired, love magic. This last, when used in moderation to attract a partner, may be quite acceptable and is only condemned when turned to incestuous or other evil purpose.

Apache witches learn their techniques by serving an apprenticeship under an older, established hand. For such occult knowledge, they must pay a substantial sum, but this is done willingly since they may expect to profit accordingly. Like their Navajo cousins, they prowl about at night and rendezvous in remote places to conduct profane rites. However, unlike Navajo witches who leave no sign when they travel,

Apache miscreants make recognizable shallow impressions in the soil.[21]

From the Mescalero Apache, one of the branches of the eastern division of the tribe beyond the Rio Grande, comes an account that shows a characteristic mode of treatment for a witch-caused ailment. A handsome youth in his late teens inexplicably became ill and took to his bed. The mother visited a famous shaman, or medicine man, and engaged him to heal her son. The physician came and after an examination announced the boy had a witch weapon in his body of such power that anyone who tried to withdraw it would die. To the Apache way of belief, a curer may succeed in removing a foreign missile or object and shooting it back to the witch, who then dies. Yet the supremacy of the former is never assured, and if the witch discovers any weak link in his medicine he can turn the tables and take revenge.

In this case the shaman ascertained that the youth had been bewitched because of his good looks and that while his medicine was potent enough to effect a cure and protect himself from death, he, nevertheless, would lose one of his own eyes for intervening in the case. With this gloomy prediction, he commenced a series of sacred songs in preparation for the removal of the witch weapon.

After the fourth song, the shaman approached the boy, began to suck on his head, and after much labor pulled out a strange object. It was a bone in the shape of an arrow, painted blue on the shaft and red at the tip, with four strands of human hair wrapped about it. Knowing that only fire could destroy such a horrible thing, he cast it into the flames, and the arrow exploded with a sound like a gunshot. By the noise the family knew that the evil object had been deactivated. In the same manner when the Mescaleros burned witches, they burst with a loud sound in the midst of the blaze, signifying that the witchcraft principle within them had been consumed.

Unfortunately the shaman in this instance had to acknowledge that another festering arrow was still lodged in his patient, and despite the most fervent ministrations he was unable to root it out. The boy finally died as a result of this second witch weapon, and the medicine man's eye, just as he had foretold, popped out. Because of the patch he wore thereafter, he was known by the name Eye-Covered.[22]

For the Apache and Navajo, supernatural phenomena emanating from the mysterious well of witchcraft disturb the order of the universe and render precarious the lives of men. Disruption of social equilibrium and development of individual trauma and anxiety that spring from this belief erode the harmony which the Indian continually seeks with his surroundings and place him at a serious disadvantage in adjusting to the world. Persons dedicated to witchcraft are, therefore, among the most monstrous enemies of mankind.

10

Herbalism and Black Magic

FROM BROWNSVILLE ON THE Gulf of Mexico to the Colorado border, desert plants and shrubs play a conspicuous role in Rio Grande witchcraft. Herbs of extraordinary properties are used in a wide variety of healing procedures and in decoctions for the removal of hexes and spells. But some go into the magical formulas of witches who use potions against their enemies or sell evil medicine to whomever is willing to pay.

Practically all Indians and non-Anglicized Hispanos of the Southwest know of certain plants that may be carried on the person or hidden in the home to give protection against sorcery and witchcraft. One of the most efficacious charms is a bit of the ubiquitous *calabazilla*, or "wild gourd," carried in pocket or purse to ward off evil. Marihuana, a plant that may be easily, if not legally, cultivated in gardens or fields, can be smoked, drunk, or chewed in powdered form each morning to keep witches at bay.[1] Flying demons, or *gente de chusma*, who sail about on the winds may be prevented from entering the home by marking a cross with ground mustard plant on the wall, a custom similar to that of Italian peasants who sprinkle mustard seed on the doorsill to scare away malign spirits. Crosses made of pine needles or twisted yucca fiber also serve to exclude witchery from the family hearth.

In the Old World, garlic has long been considered an effective defense against witchcraft, and in eastern Europe huge quantities of the bulb are consumed by the peasantry to guard against attacks by vampires. Many natives of the

Southwest also seem to regard the garlic as a protective agent, and this may explain their use as an amulet of *calabazilla*, which gives off a rank, garlicky odor.[2]

Another domestic plant associated with witch lore is corn. The *espigas de maíz*, "flower spikes on a cornstalk," are deemed useful weapons against bewitchment by many Hispanos. To work a cure, they burn the *espigas* with a sulphur match and mix the ashes with water, producing a medicine to be taken internally. If a witch has induced sores or open wounds, the *espiga* ashes are rubbed directly on the painful spots.[3] For the Keresan Pueblos along the Rio Grande, an ear of corn placed alongside an infant in its cradle will shield it from all assaults by supernatural means.[4] Yet these same people look upon certain varieties of brown and grey corn as *maíz de brujerías* ("witches' corn") that is best avoided.[5]

On the theory that vomiting will drive evils from the internal organs, particularly things shot into people by witches, emetic plants have an important place in the pharmacology of practitioners dedicated to lifting curses and spells. A Navajo phrased it in this way, "You must throw up, because if you don't bad things will stay in you and make you sick."[6] This tribe favors a species of penstemon for use as a purgative, and it is often administered during the training of young boys to expel evil. Besides using several plants for cathartic purposes, native New Mexicans occasionally resort to a dose of pure mercury *(asogue)* to achieve the same result.

In the 1890s a Mexican-American living in Rio Grande City, Texas, aroused the ire of a washerwoman because of his refusal to pay a five-dollar debt. The woman happened to practice a little witchcraft on the side, so for revenge she filled the debtor full of worms. A healer was called in just in time to save the afflicted man and she dosed him with an elixir composed of cancer herb, Gonzalez herb, and guayuli (wild rubber plant). This stout purge caused thirteen worms with green heads and white bodies to be expelled.[7]

A plant widely used by the Pueblo Indians and reported to serve various supernatural functions is *cachana*, also known as "witch root." This herb has not been identified by botanists, and, in fact, its source is a carefully guarded secret and its distribution strictly regulated by native medicine men. Since most of the root used by Pueblos and Hispanos is obtained from the Zia people, it is presumed to grow in the Jémez Mountains or on adjacent mesas. Those who sell it, men of the medicine societies, ask in exchange a ceremonial corn husk cigarette and the offering of a prayer. They also admonish the user to exercise extreme care since the plant may be dangerous if abused.[8] It is perhaps because of their knowledge of *cachana* that the Zias refer to the badger as a great medicine man who "digs in the ground and knows root medicines."[9]

Cachana disposes of witchery both in cures and as a preventive. The Cochití folk burn it as an incense during illness to purify the house, and if the patient dies, particles of the valuable root are placed around and inside the grave.[10] Other villages, including Taos, Jémez, San Felipe, Santo Domingo, Laguna, and Zuñi, burn witch root together with red chile seeds and salt to banish profane sicknesses. Individuals carry portions of *cachana* as a talisman in their pocket, tucked under a woven squaw belt, or in a personal medicine bag. Sacred bundles, containing a measure of the ground root, salt, powdered turquoise, and one grain of corn, may be buried near the door step both to bless the home and to provide an invisible shield by which witches are prevented from entering the family sanctuary.[11]

A Pueblo youth recently reported his involvement with a root, other than *cachana*, to which he also ascribed supernatural properties. Visiting in the hills north of Phoenix, he observed some Mexicans digging a small root covered with yellow fuzz that put forth a foot-high stem resembling the chile plant. When the Mexicans said they dried the roots and ate them for power, he decided to collect some himself and take them back to New Mexico. At home a reputed witch saw the dried roots, became excited, and offered to pay any price if the boy would sell them. After refusing several valuable items, the youth finally accepted in exchange a medicine bundle prepared by the witch and containing a piece of the herb. This charm was intended to bring him good luck and satisfy his every wish. Instead, after a few days he became apprehensive, especially when he placed his hand on the bundle and felt movement within. So he tied a rock on the charm and cast it into the river. A medicine man subsequently informed him that he had followed the correct procedure in disposing of the evil object in the water, for if he had buried it, the supernatural power would have remained active and tormented him the rest of his life.[12]

An unlikely plant that has become intermingled with witch practices along the Rio Grande is *cañutilla*, or "rush-circle," a prolific reed found at the river's edge and in marshes where water has overflowed. The Piros of El Paso, originally a Pueblo people who moved south at the time of the 1680 revolt, viewed *cañutilla* as a necessary adjunct to witchcraft activities and gathered quantities of the reed for various occult uses. Bundles of these they stored over main entrance ways or hung in corners of rooms, and with this evidence of their sorcery so plainly visible many Hispanos as well as other Indians shunned invitations to enter Piro houses. In the feather dance, an act of witchcraft, sorcerers of the community assembled in a kiva wearing wreaths of *cañutilla* around their heads. During the ritual they caused six or seven feathers to stand upright and dance, while they tortured and punched with needles small dolls made of corkwood, representing persons they meant to injure.[13]

Drug plants known to Indian and Mexican witches were utilized for their magical powers and as aids in supernatural acts. The most legendary were datura and peyote. Aztecs consumed both of these to produce visions and facilitate communication with the gods. Under the influence of one or the other, native priests divined the cause of illness and identified culpable witches.[14] This was the case not only among the Indians of central Mexico, but also among the Zuñi and other Pueblos in the upper Rio Grande Valley.[15]

Herbal summaries in the ancient Aztec codices speak of datura, called *ololiuhqui* (corrupted in Spanish to *toloache*), as the plant that intoxicates, makes the head swim, and bewitches one. By secretly placing a bit of the narcotic in a person's food or water, sorcerers could cause dizziness and terrifying hallucinations. Some of the same result was achieved with peyote, described by the sixteenth century Florentine Codex as "found only in the stony expanse called the Region of the Dead," that is, the desert of northern Mexico. According to this source, "Upon him who eats or drinks it, peyote produces an effect similar to that of the mushroom. He sees many startling or amusing things. For one day, perhaps two, he feels the effects; then they pass. But it damages the heart; disturbs people; intoxicates them; makes them demented."[16]

In historic times two north Mexican tribes, the Huichol of Nayarit and the Tarahumara inhabiting the Sierra Madre, have made extensive use of peyote in religious rites. Since the small cactuslike plant is native to neither area, both peoples must undertake arduous pilgrimages, which they surround with much ceremony, to the northern deserts where it grows. Huichol peyote-seekers journey on foot forty-three days to San Luís Potosí to make their collection, while the Tarahumaras venture into the Chihuahuan Desert toward the Rio Grande searching for a supply of the plant.[17] The latter group identifies peyote as one of its gods, the most powerful of herbs, and the cure for maladies and bewitchment when all else has failed.[18]

The ritual use of peyote among Indians of the United States, especially as it pertained to the development of nativistic cults and the Ghost Dance religion of the late 1800s, has engaged the attention of numerous writers and scholars.[19] In their investigations, they have demonstrated how the hallucinogenic plant was traded and spread across the Rio Grande to the Pueblo and southern Plains people and eventually became known to most tribes in the American West. But practically all have missed the fact that peyote was familiar to and used by both Indians and Spaniards in New Mexico as early as the mid-1600s, when it was employed as an aid in divination, witchery, and other occult practices.

It is quite apparent that peyote and the lore associated with it were introduced by Aztec servants and retainers who accompanied Spanish colonists to the northern frontier. Once the Pueblos became familiar with the wonders of the plant, however, some individuals on their own initiative appear to have traveled to the lower Rio Grande to gather a supply.

In the spring of 1631, Ana Cadimo, a resident of Santa Fe, denounced herself before a representative of the Inquisition, claiming that she had been led astray by an Aztec herbalist named Francisca Sombrerero. According to her statement, she had been suffering a case of bewitchment, for which Francisca had prescribed peyote. By taking the drug, it was promised that the identity of the witch would become known and the narcotic effect would guarantee a cure. Since the herbalist herself had none of the plant, Cadimo secured the necessary quantity from an old Indian of San Marcos Pueblo. Unfortunately, as she admitted in her declaration, after taking crushed peyote in water her health did not improve nor did she learn the name of the witch who had attacked her.

In another case from the same period, a mulatto, Juan Anton, came to the attention of Inquisition authorities because he recommended that peyote be used to heal a broken arm. He further stated that the herb was helpful in locating lost objects and related that once in Chihuahua, after taking a potion of six or seven peyote roots ground to powder and mixed with water, he received a vision that allowed him to recover a bundle of stolen clothes.[20] The Church, of course, took exception to claims such as these and conducted investigations because of the suggestion of heresy, devil worship, or witchcraft, all of which constituted crimes against religion.

Evidently some peyote continued to be used in New Mexico during the eighteenth century — its presence was noted briefly at Taos and Isleta Pueblos, for example — but with decreasing frequency, primarily because of the lack of a local source. Indeed, by the time the Anglo-Americans reached the

Rio Grande, the drug had been largely forgotten. Only after 1900 with the rise of the Native American Church, which has an elaborate peyote ritual as its core, did the plant again win a place in southwestern folk culture.

Unlike peyote, which grows only in a narrow belt across northern Mexico, datura may be found at elevations above one thousand feet from western Texas to California. Known also as thorn apple and jimson weed, this plant is deceptively handsome with its white, bell-shaped flowers and silver-grey leaves. All portions of the herb are poisonous if taken in large doses since they contain the potent alkaloid atropine, but most native medicine men of the Southwest knew techniques that allowed them to administer datura for medicinal purposes and to use its narcotic properties to induce dreams and visions in religious ceremonies.

The Indians of Sandía Pueblo north of Albuquerque believe the datura flower may be "shot" into persons by witches, in the same manner as a stone, cactus needle, or other object, and that it may be withdrawn by a healer following accepted procedures.[21] Zuñi medicine men partake of the vision-producing datura in an effort to locate witch objects inside their patients, and under its trancelike spell they may foretell future events.

An old Zuñi tradition tells of a boy and girl dwelling in the underworld who found a trail leading up to the world of light. They emerged wearing garlands of datura flowers on their heads, permitting them to put people to sleep and make them see ghosts. Yet this herb-derived power proved their undoing, for the gods became alarmed and sent them back to the world of darkness. But where they vanished the same white blossoms that had adorned their hair sprang forth on a vine and soon spread across the far deserts and mesas.[22]

Some Pueblo Indians employed portions of the datura as a primitive anesthetic, while others ground flowers and roots to prepare a salve for bruises and wounds.[23] With so much potency concentrated in a single plant, it is not surprising that those with evil intentions found it a convenient helpmate.

Witches, both Spanish and Indian, harvested and dried datura to stock their herb cupboards, and when a poison was called for they put some in a broth, together with fangs of a rattlesnake. The resulting concoction could be dispensed in lethal doses, or, given in moderation, it served to scare a faithless lover to repentance.[24]

The Navajos consume a tiny portion of datura as protection against witchcraft, although other herbs in their pharmacopoeia such as "witch plant" and "lightning herb" bring the same result. Because of its strength, datura must always be administered with extreme caution, and, in fact, many Navajo physicians are afraid to prescribe it. Those not so inhibited use it under the theory that any patient having the hardihood to take such powerful and dangerous medicine may easily withstand all forms of natural or supernatural attack.[25] Yet the Navajos possess many stories concerning persons gone crazy through injudicious consumption of the narcotic, and for the majority it is clearly a plant they would prefer to avoid.

In one small area of Navajoland, the region extending from the eastern slope of the Lukachukai Mountains to Ganado, Arizona, a handful of practitioners engage in datura divination; that is, they utilize the plant to trace thieves and find misplaced objects. In one instance a family had lost a valuable string of turquoise beads and an old man, familiar with medicinal plants and herbs, agreed to recover it. He gave a young boy a handful of datura and bade him chew it up. The youngster went out of his mind, dashed from the hogan, and began circling the sheep corral. A crowd that gathered watched him take up a stick and begin poking through manure inside the fence. In a short while he dug up the string of missing beads, and the old man quickly fed him an antidote that brought back his sanity.[26]

Around the turn of the present century, the most notorious witch and herb doctor in the Santa Fe district was Dolores la Penca, whose very name was used by parents to terrify mischievous children. "La Penca" in Spanish means "the found-

PLATE 8. *Blooming sacred datura, a narcotic plant favored by southwestern witches.*

ling" and referred to the fact that Dolores had been abandoned as an infant and raised by a foster family. Even as a child, she caused people to remark upon her mysterious behavior, and by her late teens she left home and went to live alone in a small adobe on the Agua Fria Road. Often for weeks at a time, Dolores la Penca roamed the nearby Sangre de Cristo Mountains collecting medicinal plants and herbs to serve as the principal ingredients in her broths, potions, and spells of enchantment. She occasionally traded with sheepherders for a rare flower or bush that she could not find in her own solitary wanderings. Those who dared enter her humble mud house reported in awe-filled tones that the interior was adorned with the evidence of her strange trade — hoofs and horns and bunches of dried herbs festooning the rafters, and bags of leaves piled on the floor.

For years Dolores la Penca was a source of deep anxiety for the Hispano folk of her neighborhood, until finally the evil she dispensed was turned against her, as may happen to any witch. A young girl was about to be married and Dolores took her a gift — a bar of homemade soap with an odd but engagingly sweet smell. The girl's mother warned her against using it, but the odor was so beguiling she washed her hair with the soap that same night. On the following day the bride-to-be broke out with a terrible red rash, and she became frightened that a spell had been cast upon her marriage. "Who wants to enter their wedding day," she wailed, "looking like a smallpox victim?" And yet on the day of the ceremony, the rash inexplicably disappeared.

The week she was to be married, the bride's brother and cousin were away working with a survey party in southern New Mexico. Shortly afterward, the pair returned and related a strange tale. On the day of the wedding, the brother sat by the campfire thinking of the festivities and wishing he could be in Santa Fe. Suddenly an owl began to hoot in the piñon trees close by, and the cousin, Antonio, remarked, "Ah, there is Dolores la Penca. She has come all this way looking for trouble or for news to carry back to Santa Fe."

When the brother appeared incredulous, Antonio continued, "Witches can take any form and travel hundreds of miles in no time. Dolores has come as that owl, and you watch and see if I am not right." Then taking out his rifle, he marked a cross on the bullet and killed the owl with a shot through the eye. Going to examine the bird, they found the right eye gone, the left wing raised and almost torn off, and the left foot doubled up under the small body.

On returning home, the two young men stopped at the adobe of Dolores la Penca, but found it vacant and the door locked. Proceeding to the home of the new bride to offer congratulations, they inquired about the witch woman, and learned that she was dead — slain mysteriously on the very night of the wedding. A sheepherder bringing herbs had been the last to see her alive. On the following morning a neighbor had called, observed the locked door, and broken in to discover the mangled body. Dolores, the witch, was lying on the floor, a bullet through her right eye, her left arm raised and practically torn loose, and her foot doubled up against her chest. The two youths exchanged glances and made the sign of the cross as they recalled the bullet that ended an owl's life and at the same time closed the career of Santa Fe's most infamous herbalist.[27]

In the Southwest Hispano practitioners who make use of medicinal herbs may be divided loosely into two categories: *curanderos* ("healers") and witch doctors (called *arbularios* in New Mexico). The many persons dispensing beneficial plants for curing purposes vary from knowledgeable housewives who may treat friends and neighbors with a few favorite remedies, to the professional herbal physicians whose insight and abilities are believed to be gifts endowed by God. All genuine *curanderos* scrupulously avoid anything that smacks of black magic, since the progress of their work depends in large measure upon confidence placed in them by patients. Most of them out of self-defense refuse to treat cases of bewitchment, because success would imply that they had intimate knowledge of dark supernatural power.

Don Pedro Jaramillo, until his death in 1907, was the best known sage and healer ministering in the country drained by the Rio Grande. He lived on Los Olmos Ranch in Starr County, Texas, and received patients from as far away as Socorro, New Mexico. His prescriptions were given without charge, but the simple folk paid what they could, many claiming they were beneficiaries of almost miraculous cures. In only one instance was Don Pedro known to have relented and tried to undo a case of bewitchment. A young woman under a spell that caused her to have seizures and convulsions sought his aid, but in spite of his most careful attention he could provide her no relief. She later perished when she fell into the fire during an attack and was burned to death.[28]

Healing specialists, treating folk ills with herbs, remain popular among the large Mexican-American population of southern Texas and New Mexico.[29] But alongside them may also be found persons who combine the arts of curing and black magic, and who for want of a better term are called witch doctors. As a matter of routine they distribute herb charms and deal in drug plants, such as datura or marihuana, that produce hallucinations and vascular excitement. Unlike the *curanderos*, they demand substantial payment for their services, either in cash or gifts.

Many people, of course, are too fearful to consult a witch doctor, since most, like the hapless Dolores la Penca of Santa Fe, inspire only the profoundest dread. Yet a very strong belief, extending back to medieval Spain, persists that sorcerers who can join healing with magic are sometimes the only source for a workable remedy.[30] Recently a Hispano woman in El Paso, who had spent seven years in a hospital without her illness showing improvement, decided to consult a witch doctor. He treated her by brushing her nude body with a broom made of common garden flowers, and thereafter she made a rapid recovery.[31]

Since *curanderos* generally resist treating maladies arising from any form of enchantment, a patient's only recourse may be that of seeking the services of a witch doctor. The theory prevails that some stubborn spells respond only to exorcism by another witch. A man in northern New Mexico had taken his son, Carpio, to several doctors but none had been able to discover an organic cause for his strange ailment. At times the boy could be found crouching in the corner of his room and crying that a woman in a black shawl had pricked him with cactus needles. The worried father eventually consulted a "smart witch," renowned as a diagnostician, and she agreed to work a cure. But she advised the man to exercise the utmost secrecy, "because if the other witches catch me they will give me a good licking!"

At the old woman's request, Carpio, a new copper kettle, and a huge sunflower were deposited at her house. She cast a handful of herbs into the pot along with the flower and set it to brew in the corner fireplace. Preparing for the night, she locked and barred the door, curtained the windows, and swept the coals and ashes from the fireplace before placing on the hearth a statue of Saint Cirilio, who is invoked for protection against witchery. At last she had the boy drink a cup of the herb and sunflower broth.

During the night Carpio heard noises at the door and windows as if someone was trying to gain entry, and the sound of hooting and flapping of wings issued from the chimney top. A bucket of water cascaded down the smokehole, but when he lighted a candle all became quiet. The same scene was reenacted the next night, but Saint Cirilio maintained his guard over the only opening into the house, and the prowling witches could not get in. On the third day the father came, collected his son, and took him home cured.[32]

Occasionally, a witch who brings a curse on someone may be implored or even hired to remove the evil. According to a New Mexican folk tale, a witch of Galisteo known as Tia Sarquita brought misery in one guise or another to most of the members of the community, usually by means of herbs or potions. Once she gave a woman bewitched watermelon seeds, and when planted they bore tempting fruit. The woman ate one of the melons and little by little began to grow sick. By

April of the following year a strange growth appeared on her breast, and she knew only that Tia Sarquita was the source of her infirmity. The witch came and, after being prodded, recommended that the sufferer kill a dog and bathe her body in the blood. The poor woman submitted to this grisly ritual, but still her health did not return, nor did the growth disappear. The witch then came and anointed her with a plaster composed of herbs, soap, and gum, which caused watermelon juice to drop from her body, and she was healed.[33]

When a case of bewitchment has been diagnosed by either a Hispano or Indian practitioner, removal of the hex may be undertaken, as we have seen earlier, by any of a variety of procedures, the use of healing or hallucinogenic herbs constituting only a single trick in the curer's bag of lore. But because of the profusion and accessibility of exotic plants throughout the mountains and deserts of the Southwest, herbalism should continue to flourish as long as folk medicine and witchcraft command a significant following.

11

The Lingering Legacy of Witchcraft

IN THE SPRING OF 1956, police in Las Cruces, New Mexico, answered a call from a hysterical woman, who claimed she had returned home that evening to find evidence of witchcraft on her front step. When officers arrived, she showed them a pile of sulphur against the door and a burnt match pointing toward her bedroom. Two packets of needles lay on the step, with a single needle laid across the rest to form an X. The woman tearfully reported that a former business partner had become jealous two months before and had declared "I'll fix you," while scattering white powder on the ground. A week later someone broke into her home and beat her, other ill luck had followed, and now here was confirmation of the spell placed upon her. As newspaper photographers snapped away with their cameras, the police removed the hex material. Yet notwithstanding this official purging of the premises, the distraught victim announced firmly she would not spend another night in her house.[1]

Erna Fergusson wrote in the mid-1940s that witches were still active and were occasionally apprehended in southwestern villages, but that education was fast destroying their power.[2] While this remains true in the 1970s, belief in witchcraft yet shows signs of vigorous life and its influence will undoubtedly be felt for a long time to come. Faith in the occult arts continues not only among rural folk, but as the case above illustrates, among presumably more sophisticated urban residents. In fact, when Wesley R. Hurt surveyed the subject several years ago, he found practices of witchery stronger in Bernalillo, a large community on the Rio Grande near Albuquerque, than in the isolated mountain village of Manzano.[3]

The Las Cruces incident also demonstrates that people still believe an attack upon them by witches legitimately comes under the jurisdiction of the legal authorities. In 1966 when the Alfares Quintana home in El Llano, south of Taos, came under supernatural assault, the family summoned the State Police. Repeatedly a barrage of rocks pelted the house during the late night hours, and some observers claimed to have seen weird bouncing lights. The wife of Ambrose Mascarenas, the local justice of the peace, described fireballs "about the size of a golfball, strange in color, bluish or grey, not at all like a flashlight. They bounced along higher than a man's head, and disappeared into the trees farther down the Santa Barbara River."[4]

Townspeople as well as police kept a night vigil armed with guns and lanterns, but sailing rocks pierced the tight cordon anyway, and thumped against the Quintana house. A hail of bullets fired into the darkness seemed to have little effect, and searches of the area produced no trace of intruders, not even footprints. Some village residents reportedly took the precaution of turning their clothes inside out and marking crosses on the bullets going into their rifles. State Police Sgt. Simon Doitchinoff, head of the Taos district office, who visited the scene, commented on the mystery: "I just don't know what or who it is. If I did, I'd sure catch them. It's very strange, for the Quintanas are fine people and give no trouble to anyone."[5] The family, indeed, disclaimed belief in supernatural agents as the cause of its misfortune, although the details of the episode show that it was clearly within the classic pattern of Rio Grande witch lore.

In the predominantly Mexican-American communities of south Texas emphasis on occultism today revolves around a variety of folk ailments believed to be supernaturally inspired. *Mal puesto* ("artificially induced illness"), *mal ojo* (the ubiquitous "evil eye"), and *susto* (a malady produced by "witch fright") all fall within the realm of the Devil and require supernatural remedies, usually by *curanderos*, to exorcise the evil. But here too, crimes traceable to witchcraft may be brought to the attention of minions of the law. One Latin expressed it in this way. "Witches hide their identity from the Christians and the police. And well they should. If we could name them, we would round them up and destroy them. They are Satan's children and our enemies."[6]

In New Mexico and southern Colorado, contemporary witchcraft belief persists in the traditional, archaic mold, retaining its own distinctive and highly provincial tone. But on the lower Rio Grande, and below San Antonio, an infusion of traits and practices from Old Mexico continues to build innumerable links between witches along the border and their fraternal kinsmen farther south. Some persons wishing to engage the services or obtain charms of an especially potent practitioner of the black arts may travel as far as the Valley of Mexico or the city of Guadalajara in their quest. By the same token, healers of well-known reputation may be sought south of the Rio Grande and their formulas for spell-lifting purchased with American dollars.

A story current among the villagers north of Albuquerque tells of a native of Mexico who wandered up from the border and established a "witchcraft practice" in Bernalillo. His foreign ways of sorcery appeared strange to the local people, particularly his reliance upon a *Libro Negro*, or "Black Book," that furnished arcane information. A man desiring to become his apprentice went to him and asked for instruction. The witch agreed and told him that if he aspired to enter the world of black magic, he must pass three tests. Suddenly sprouting wings, the witch grabbed the man and flew away to a witches' party. Here the student was obliged to kiss a goat, then a snake, but failed the last test requiring that he join in feasting upon a cadaver. On exclaiming holy words, the man saw that the bestial festivities had vanished from view, and he found himself alone but wiser in the wilderness.

As we have seen, this was a standard folk tale associated with witchery from Antonito, Colorado, as far south as San Elizario, Texas. The only variation in this case was provided by the witch from Old Mexico who consulted his Black Book and grew a pair of wings.[7]

One aspect of belief which we have not dwelled upon before and which retains many adherents throughout the Southwest is that associated with the power of hens' eggs to heal supernaturally caused afflictions or otherwise counteract the evil spread by witches. Use of an egg in both diagnosing and curing is an ancient folk remedy, and its retention even today may well be due to the ease of application, which requires only simple procedures administered discreetly in the home. One technique involves rubbing the patient with whole eggs so that their white purity draws the power of the witch out of his body. A treatment popular everywhere in New Mexico for hangovers or any type of nausea, whether linkable to witches or not, prescribes that an egg be rubbed on the stomach, then broken and poured into a saucer which is placed behind the patient's head.[8] The cleansing qualities of eggs serve in a similar manner to rescue a child from bewitchment, particularly a case of *mal ojo*. A yoke and egg white are emptied into a bowl and set on a chair beside the sleeping youngster, an eye soon appears in the bowl, and he is healed.

A rural mother in one of the south Texas counties, who professed disbelief in superstition, nevertheless recalled a few years ago that when her infant became feverish and fretful she resorted to an egg in an effort to find the cause. Dropping the yoke in a glass of water, she saw it take a shape she knew was the diagnostic criterion for *mal ojo*. Satisfied with this revelation, she massaged the child with whole hens' eggs, made the sign of the cross, recited three prayers, and from then on the trouble disappeared.[9] A somewhat more bizarre result was reported by a *curandero* who seated his patient on a stool and set under it a broken egg in a saucer. He next performed his healing rites as an antidote to the witch poison, causing the evil to strike down so hotly through the stool that it cooked the egg.[10]

As already suggested, many believers in witchcraft are reluctant to discuss their experiences with outsiders for fear of being scorned or subjected to ridicule. On those infrequent occasions when they are led to relate some incident involving the supernatural, a paradoxical qualification may preface their remarks, such as the one given by an old resident of Albuquerque: "Of course, I don't believe this story, but it happened just as I'm going to describe it."[11] Tellers of witch tales in Manzano protect themselves by announcing this clear reservation: "My uncle (or some other person) told me this story when I was a boy. There may have been witches a long time ago, but I have never seen one myself."[12] This current skepticism plainly serves as a defense mechanism and has grown up only in recent decades as a hostile public attitude developed toward belief in witchcraft. This was distinctly not the case in the 1890s when Lt. John G. Bourke interviewed a young Hispano woman who emphatically proclaimed that witches were all around "taking delight in doing harm to you personally, or in spreading sickness among your cattle, or blighting your crops and fruit trees."[13]

Many modern Hispanos and Indians, although convinced of the reality of witchcraft, believe that its use is on the wane. One Pueblo man expressed his sentiments in this way. "Since about 1930 the medicine men don't go out from the village to hunt witches. They are afraid to be seen by the Whites. Today, the witches do things to be mean, that's all. We already have been breaking up the witches. Maybe we caught most of them."[14]

Madsen, writing of the Mexican-Americans in the lower Rio Grande Valley, contends that there, belief in witchcraft remains strongest among adult members of the lower and lower-middle classes, while the elite and anglicized representatives of the upper class dismiss it as superstition of the lowly and uneducated people. A concerted attack upon all forms of witchcraft in the press, the schools, and the churches helps to discredit its practice, but by no means eliminates it as a festering sore upon the still extensive body of Hispanic folk culture.[15]

While the censure of Anglos tends to discourage open conversation regarding witches, dangers inherent in the nature of the subject itself work to the same end. Experts in black magic can become invisible or transform themselves into a bird or animal and in this way hover nearby undetected, listen secretly to conversations, and gather evidence against those who may discuss witchcraft too freely or speak of it in critical terms. Silence, therefore, is practically mandatory for timid believers. The vast knowledge accumulated by witches through constant alertness is proverbial, and explains the meaning of the traditional Spanish saying *Es como los brujos, duerme con los ojos abiertos* ("He is like the witches, for he sleeps with his eyes open").[16]

Although faith in witchcraft seems to be declining among economically advantaged Hispanos and among better educated Pueblo Indians, the seeds of belief continue to flourish in the Navajo population. Clyde Kluckhohn noted that Navajo friends who at first resolutely denied the very existence of witchcraft, later gaining his confidence, poured forth deep-seated fears and admitted detailed experiences with the occult. Over a twenty-year period and through remarkable persistence, he was able to interview nineteen persons widely rumored to be witches and three others who had actually been "tried" for witchcraft.[17] From the data he collected, it is apparent that theories of witchery still hold the Navajos in a steely grip, and will continue to do so in the foreseeable future.

In surveying popular notions of supernaturalism prevalent along the Rio Grande, this book has dwelled upon the history and practice of witchcraft, but it should be made clear that other grotesque or odd beliefs hold the common folk in bondage. One of these is the fear of ghosts *(los difuntos)*, as strong among some sectors of the Hispano community as among the Navajos. A plethora of superstitions is attached to death and the inescapability of its consequences receives affirmation in the refrain *De la muerte y de la suerte nadie se escape* ("Death and destiny no one can avoid"). An instinctive horror attaches to the departed, and young and old alike among the living fear to go alone into the dark lest they encounter a ghost. And unfortunate is the family once visited by death, for more deaths swiftly and inexorably follow.[18]

Other members of the spirit world who invoke terror are *los duendes* ("dwarfs"), individuals of small stature dedicated to frightening the lazy, the wicked, and especially the filthy. *Los duendes* inhabit dark regions underground and emerge at night to steal provisions or clothing and bedevil delinquent humans. In this they resemble both the dwarfs of Celtic myth who lived in black caves, and the demons of the Middle Ages who swarmed in the night air seeking men and women to torment.[19] In New Mexican folklore, the *duendes* originated at the time Lucifer was cast out of heaven. So many angels followed him that God feared none would remain in his own choir, so he slammed the gates leaving a multitude of winged seraphs suspended between heaven and hell. With no place to go, these abandoned angels became dwarfs living in limbo. In the Rio Grande settlements, they flit about as mischievous little spirits, occupying vacant houses and throwing pebbles from the rooftops at passing people. Occasionally they seize possession of newlybuilt houses, annoying the residents at night with all manner of pranks and queer noises. They move furniture around with loud scraping and thudding, and the next morning people find their furnishings all out of place. And they are wanton thieves, taking anything that strikes their fancy. So invariably when Hispanos lose something, they acknowledge that *los duendes* got it.[20]

Another mythical being is the basilisk *(el basilisco)*, whose roots revert back to a fabled reptile of the African desert with a breath and look said to be fatal. In Spain and much of South America, the chimerical basilisk is a snake born from an egg laid by a cock, but in our own Southwest the creature issues directly from a hen and is not a serpent at all, but a shapeless, ugly form, jet black, and resembling an ill-made chick. Actually in this region, any female bird or fowl may give birth to a basilisk. As to the deadly effect of the monster's eye, the Rio Grande myth follows belief in other parts of the world. If the basilisk sees someone first, that person dies; but, if the situation is reversed and the creature is caught unaware and observed by a human first, then it dies. Once a basilisk found a home in a magpie's nest along a New Mexico road, and many unsuspecting people traveling by were killed by its deadly gaze. Finally a mirror was placed near the nest; the beast looked at its own reflection, and perished. The same story, with slight variations, occurs in such widely separated places as Chile, France, and Spain.[21]

Throughout the Southwest one may find evidence of the legend of *La Llorona*, "the Weeping Woman," represented in some instances as an old witch, and in others as a lost soul from purgatory. At times she may still be met at late hours in the streets of Santa Fe, dressed in black, dragging heavy chains, and bitterly crying. When she is heard at the door, no one dares leave the house, for her presence is a certain harbinger of tragedy. In Texas, *La Llorona* is sometimes pictured as a repentant mother, who weeps because she drowned her naughty children in a fit of anger. School children, even today, in Las Vegas, New Mexico, are warned by parents to beware of the wailing apparition, for she tries to steal youngsters to replace her own lost progeny.[22] Farming folk around Tomé, south of Albuquerque, contend that the tearful ghost is not a witch, but the spirit of a young maiden who jumped off a mountain top when jilted by her lover. Yet, other Hispanos know her as a dealer in witchcraft, possessed of power to change people into frogs.

The tale of *La Llorona* is a familiar one in the folk literature of Spain, but as related along the Rio Grande, it also shows traces suggesting Aztec mythology. Tonantzin, an Aztec goddess, mixed among native women snatching babies from their cradles and leaving an arrowhead shaped like a sacrificial knife in their place. At night she roamed through Aztec towns shrieking and weeping, disappearing with dawn into the waters of lakes or rivers.[23] At least forty-two different versions of the story have been collected from the Southwest, and there is scarcely a person of Hispanic origin who does not have some acquaintance with this doleful lady.[24]

As our previous discussion has shown, much attention is given herbs, in the curing of both witch-caused ailments and folk illnesses. Remedies using other agents, however, are universally employed and compose an important part of superstitious belief. To stop a nosebleed, a wet key or coin is pressed to the forehead. Cutting hair by a full moon makes it grow faster. A glass of water placed on the head of a patient suffering from sunstroke soon begins to boil and results in a cure. Chapped hands may be softened by washing them in the urine of a male child. When horses have the colic, they should be wrapped in the skirts of a woman who has just given birth. Removal of warts may be accomplished by standing under a rainbow and tying a hair around the swelling, for as the rainbow disappears, so will the wart. And to alleviate tonsilitis, sufferers jerk their fingers until the knuckles pop.[25] These and similar palliatives continue in the twentieth century to serve the needs of those of simple faith, not only because they are encrusted with tradition, but because they are, for both rural and urban poor, far cheaper than the services of a physician.

It is quite easy, and indeed fashionable, for modern man to dismiss folk medicine, witchcraft, and other forms of supernaturalism as unadulterated humbuggery, and yet who at present is so well versed in all things that he can pretend to know the extent of the power of belief.

Notes

Introduction
1. "Bewitched," *Santa Fe New Mexican*, September 24, 1972.

Chapter 1: A Dark Heritage
1. Clyde Kluckhohn, *Navajo Witchcraft* (Boston, 1967), p. 72.
2. Chadwick Hansen, *Witchcraft at Salem* (New York, 1969), pp. 4–5.
3. See her *The God of the Witches* (London, 1933).
4. Ronald Seth, *Witches and Their Craft* (New York, 1968), p. 96.
5. Quoted in *Ibid.*, p. 73.
6. Charles Mackay, *Extraordinary Popular Delusions and the Madness of Crowds* (New York, 1932), p. 480.
7. *Ibid.*, p. 481.
8. A reappraisal of the Massachusetts episode is provided by Hansen, *Witchcraft at Salem.*
9. Seth, *Witches and Their Craft*, p. 87.
10. George A. Dorsey, *Man's Own Show: Civilization* (New York, 1931), p. 594.
11. Henry Kamen, *The Spanish Inquisition* (New York, 1965), p. 205; and Arántzazu Hurtado de Saracho, *Medicina Popular de Navarra* (Pamplona, 1968), pp. 12–13.
12. Cecil Roth, *The Spanish Inquisition* (New York, 1964), p. 201.
13. Kamen, *The Spanish Inquisition*, p. 209; and A. S. Tuberville, *La Inquisición Española* (Mexico, 1948), p. 105.
14. William and Claudia Madsen, *A Guide to Mexican Witchcraft* (Mexico, 1969), p. 10.
15. Lewis Hanke, *Aristotle and the American Indians* (Chicago, 1959), p. 4.
16. Frans Blom, *The Conquest of Yucatan* (Boston, 1936), pp. 123, 127.
17. Madsen, *Guide to Mexican Witchcraft*, pp. 10–11.
·18. George C. Vaillant, *The Aztecs of Mexico* (Baltimore, 1944), pp. 231–33.

19. Madsen, *Guide to Mexican Witchcraft*, p. 12.

20. See Edward S. Gifford, Jr., *The Evil Eye, Studies in the Folklore of Vision* (New York, 1958).

21. Elsie C. Parsons, *Mitla: Town of the Souls* (Chicago, 1936), p. 251.

22. Frances Toor, *A Treasury of Mexican Folkways* (New York, 1947), p. 155.

23. For an example see Ralph L. Beals, *Cherán: A Sierra Tarascan Village* (Washington, D.C., 1946), pp. 156–61.

Chapter 2: The Devil's Domain on the Rio Grande

1. George P. Hammond and Agapito Rey, eds., *The Rediscovery of New Mexico: 1580–1594* (Albuquerque, 1966), p. 100.

2. George P. Hammond and Agapito Rey, eds., *Fray Alonso de Benavides' Revised Memorial of 1634* (Albuquerque, 1945), p. 45.

3. Frederick Webb Hodge and Charles Fletcher Lummis, eds., *The Memorial of Fray Alonso de Benavides, 1630* (Chicago, 1916), p. 26.

4. France V. Sholes, "The First Decade of the Inquisition in New Mexico," *New Mexico Historical Review*, 10 (1935):208–14.

5. *Ibid.*, p. 218.

6. *Ibid.*, pp. 220–22; and Fray Angélico Chávez, *Origins of New Mexico Families* (Santa Fe, 1954), p. 69.

7. Seth, *Witches and Their Craft*, p. 117.

8. Kurt Seligmann, *Magic, Supernaturalism, and Religion* (New York, 1968), p. 219.

9. Documents concerning the Gruber case have been translated in Charles Wilson Hackett and Charmion C. Chelby, eds. and trans., *Historical Documents Relating to New Mexico, Nueva Vizcaya, and Approaches Thereto, to 1773*, 3 vols. (Washington, D.C., 1923–37), 3:271–77.

10. Hubert Howe Bancroft, *History of Arizona and New Mexico* (San Francisco, 1889), p. 175.

11. Fray Angélico Chávez, "Pohé-yemo's Representative and the Pueblo Revolt of 1680," *New Mexico Historical Review*, 42 (1967): 85–95.

12. *Spanish Archives of New Mexico*, II, doc. no. 137b, "Trial of Catherina Lujan, et al.," May 13–31, 1708, State Records Center, Santa Fe (cited hereinafter as *SANM*).

13. *SANM*, II, doc. no. 381, "Trial Record of Isleta Indians Charged with Witchcraft," February 11–19, 1733. This case is summarized in Tibo J. Chávez, "Early Witchcraft in New Mexico," *El Palacio*, 77 (1970):7–9.

14. Ralph Emerson Twitchell, *The Leading Facts of New Mexican History*, 2 vols. (Albuquerque, 1963), I, pp. 445–46; and Eleanor B. Adams and Fray Angélico Chávez, eds., *The Missions of New Mexico, 1776* (Albuquerque, 1956), p. 336. After this was written a copy of the trial

record was located by Gilberto Benito Cordova at the Bancroft Library of the University of California, Berkeley.

15. *SANM*, II, doc. no. 1394, "Case Against Indians of Sandía Pueblo," August 3–23, 1797.

16. *SANM*, II, doc. no. 1462, "Verdict of Pedro de Nava," September 11, 1799.

17. *SANM*, II, doc. no. 1503, "Letter of Governor Chacón to Nava," August 30, 1800. See also Fray Angélico Chávez, *Archives of the Archdiocese of Santa Fe* (Washington, D.C., 1957), p. 244.

Chapter 3: Executions and the Diabolical Kiss

1. W. W. H. Davis, *El Gringo* (Santa Fe, 1938), p. 93.

2. "Whipped for Witchcraft," *Santa Fe Daily New Mexican*, October 2, 1882.

3. "Death of a Witch," *New Mexican Review*, September 8, 1884.

4. Ruth Laughlin Barker, "New Mexico Witch Tales," in J. Frank Dobie, ed., *Tone the Bell Easy* (Austin, 1932), p. 66.

5. Anonymous, "Felicia the Witch," unpublished MS. in files of *Works Progress Administration Project*, Museum of New Mexico, Santa Fe. (Cited hereafter as *WPA Papers*.)

6. Aurelio Espinosa, "New Mexican Spanish Folklore," *Journal of American Folklore*, 23 (1910):396n.

7. Madsen, *Guide to Mexican Witchcraft*, p. 54.

8. Cleofas M. Jaramillo, *Shadows of the Past* (Santa Fe, 1972), p. 102.

9. Wesley R. Hurt, Jr., "Witchcraft in New Mexico," *El Palacio*, 47 (1940):78–79.

10. Charles F. Lummis, *A Tramp Across the Continent* (New York, 1920), pp. 196–98.

11. Juan B. Rael, ed., *Cuentos Españoles de Colorado y de Nuevo Méjico*, 2 vols. (Stanford, n.d.), 2:811–12.

12. Charles F. Lummis, *A New Mexico David* (New York, 1916), p. 132.

13. Jaramillo, *Shadows of the Past*, p. 101.

14. Barker, "New Mexico Witch Tales," pp. 63–64.

15. Hurt, "Witchcraft in New Mexico," p. 75.

16. John G. Bourke, "Superstitions of the Rio Grande," *Journal of American Folklore*, 7 (1894):143.

17. Letter of Amado Chaves to Charles F. Lummis, Santa Fe, December 5, 1897, Southwest Museum Collection, Los Angeles.

18. [Charles F. Lummis], "Witchcraft in New Mexico," *Journal of American Folklore*, 1 (1888):167.

19. Hurt, "Witchcraft in New Mexico," p. 75.

20. Jaramillo, *Shadows of the Past*, p. 103.

21. Hurt, "Witchcraft in New Mexico," pp. 80–81.

22. Rumaldita Gurule, "La Cita de las Brujas," *WPA Papers.*

23. Barker, "New Mexico Witch Tales," p. 67.

24. Lummis, *A New Mexico David*, pp. 130–31.

25. Charles F. Lummis, *Some Strange Corners of Our Country* (New York, 1892), p. 71.

26. Lummis, *A New Mexico David*, p. 125.

Chapter 4: The Ways of Witches

1. José Manuel Espinosa, *Spanish Folk-Tales from New Mexico* (New York, 1937), p. 216.

2. Charles F. Lummis, *Mesa, Cañon and Pueblo* (New York, 1925), p. 351.

3. [Lummis], "Witchcraft in New Mexico," p. 168.

4. Jaramillo, *Shadows of the Past*, p. 102.

5. Gurule, "La Cita de las Brujas." *WPA Papers.*

6. Lummis, *A New Mexico David*, p. 129.

7. Rael, *Cuentos Españoles*, 2:595.

8. Madsen, *Guide to Mexican Witchcraft*, p. 25.

9. Hurt, "Witchcraft in New Mexico," pp. 79–80.

10. Rael, *Cuentos Españoles*, 2:812–13.

11. Hurt, "Witchcraft in New Mexico,' p. 76.

12. Barker, "New Mexico Witch Tales," pp. 68–70.

13. Jaramillo, *Shadows of the Past*, p. 101.

14. Elizabeth Willis DeHuff, "Where Witches Abound," *Southwest Review*, 11 (1926):262–63.

15. Rael, *Cuentos Españoles*, 2:600–02.

16. "Felicia the Bruja," *WPA Papers.*

17. Madsen, *Guide to Mexican Witchcraft*, p. 25.

18. William Madsen, *The Mexican-Americans of South Texas* (New York, 1964), p. 84.

19. Jaramillo, *Shadows of the Past*, p. 101.

20. Lummis, *Mesa, Cañon and Pueblo*, p. 352.

21. Madsen, *Mexican-Americans*, p. 85.

22. Rael, *Cuentos Españoles*, 2:813.

23. Arthur J. Rubel, *Across the Tracks, Mexican-Americans in a Texas City* (Austin, 1966), pp. 156–61. See also by the same author, "Concepts of Disease in Mexican-American Culture," *American Anthropologist*, 42 (1960):795–814.

24. Madsen, *Mexican-Americans*, p. 76.

25. Jaramillo, *Shadows of the Past*, p. 104.

26. Hurtado de Saracho, *Medicina Popular de Navarra*, p. 12.

27. Gurule, "La Cita de las Brujas," *WPA Papers.*

28. Hurt, "Witchcraft in New Mexico," p. 78.

29. Rubel, *Across the Tracks*, p. 158.

30. Hurt, "Witchcraft in New Mexico," p. 76; and Jaramillo, *Shadows of the Past*, p. 98.

Chapter 5: Pueblo Witchcraft

1. Frederick Webb Hodge, ed., *Handbook of American Indians North of Mexico*, new printing, 2 vols. (New York, 1971), 2:966.
2. Frederick Peterson, *Ancient Mexico* (New York, 1962), p. 231.
3. Wendell C. Bennett and Robert M. Zingg, *The Tarahumara, An Indian Tribe of Northern Mexico* (Chicago, 1935), p. 264.
4. Hodge, *Handbook*, 2:966.
5. E. Adamson Hoebel, *The Cheyennes, Indians of the Great Plains* (New York, 1965), p. 88.
6. Elsie C. Parsons, *The Pueblo of Jémez* (New Haven, 1925), p. 139.
7. Alfonso Ortiz, "Ritual Drama and the Pueblo World View," in Alfonso Ortiz, ed., *New Perspectives on the Pueblos* (Albuquerque, 1972), pp. 144–45.
8. J. Robin Fox, "Witchcraft and Clanship in Cochití Therapy," in John Middleton, ed., *Magic, Witchcraft and Curing* (New York, 1967), pp. 266–68.
9. *Ibid.*, pp. 279–80.
10. Hodge, *Handbook*, 2:966.
11. Florence Hawley, "The Mechanics of Perpetuation in Pueblo Witchcraft," in Erik K. Reed and Dale S. King, eds., *For the Dean* (Santa Fe, 1950), p. 147.
12. Leslie A. White, *The Acoma Indians* (Washington, D.C., 1932), p. 123.
13. Elsie C. Parsons, *The Social Organization of the Tewa of New Mexico* (Menasha, Wisconsin, 1929), pp. 62–63.
14. White, *The Acoma Indians*, pp. 123–24.
15. Hawley, "Mechanics of Pueblo Witchcraft," p. 149.
16. DeHuff, "Where Witches Abound," p. 256.
17. *Ibid.*, p. 253.
18. *Ibid.*, pp. 255–56.
19. *Notes on Cochití, New Mexico* (Menasha, Wisconsin, 1919), p. 162.
20. Esther S. Goldfrank, *The Social and Ceremonial Organization of Cochití* (Menasha, Wisconsin, 1927), pp. 95–96.
21. Charles H. Lange and Carroll L. Riley, eds., *The Southwestern Journals of Adolph F. Bandelier, 1883–1884* (Albuquerque, 1970), p. 101.
22. Elsie C. Parsons, *Isleta* (Washington, D.C., 1932), p. 244.
23. Hawley, "Mechanics of Pueblo Witchcraft," p. 151.
24. Elsie C. Parsons, "Witchcraft Among the Pueblos: Indian or Spanish?" in Max Marwick, ed., *Witchcraft and Sorcery* (Baltimore, 1970), p. 204.
25. Parsons, *Isleta*, p. 243.

26. Goldfrank, *Social Organization of Cochití*, pp. 98–99.

27. "Witchcraft Among the Pueblos," p. 208.

28. Hawley, "Mechanics of Pueblo Witchcraft," p. 150.

29. Dennis Tedlock, "Pueblo Literature: Style and Verisimilitude," in Ortiz, *New Perspectives on the Pueblos*, p. 236.

30. Elsie C. Parsons, *Notes on Zuñi* (Menasha, Wisconsin, 1917), p. 395.

31. Goldfrank, *Social Organization of Cochití*, pp. 94–95.

32. DeHuff, "Where Witches Abound," pp. 257–58.

33. Parsons, *Isleta*, pp. 432–35.

34. Lange and Riley, *Journals of Bandelier, 1883–1884*, p. 27.

35. Matilda Coxe Stevenson, *The Zuñi Indians* (Washington, D.C., 1905), p. 403.

36 Charles H. Lange, *Cochití, A New Mexico Pueblo, Past and Present* (Austin, 1959), p. 458.

37. Goldfrank, *Social Organization of Cochití*, p. 97.

38. Lange, *Cochití*, p. 253.

39. Parsons, *Social Organization of the Tewa*, p. 62.

40. Parsons, *Isleta*, p. 205.

41. Lange, *Cochití*, p. 459.

42. Parsons, *Isleta*, p. 205.

Chapter 6: The Tragedy of Nambé

1. Davis, *El Gringo*, p. 177.

2. Frank G. Applegate, *Indian Stories from the Pueblos* (Philadelphia, 1929), pp. 97–98.

3. Adams and Chávez, *Missions of New Mexico*, p. 59.

4. *Mexican Archives of New Mexico*, "Declaration of Gaspar Ortiz," August 21, 1822, Roll 1, Frame 1294, State Records Center, Santa Fe.

5. Adolph F. Bandelier, *Final Report of Investigations Among the Indians of the Southwestern United States* (Papers of the Archeological Institute of America, 1890–1892), p. 206n. The author refers to an original manuscript then [1888] in his possession, entitled *Relacion de las Matanzas de los Brujos de Nambé* por Juan Lujan (*Account of Witch Killings at Nambé* by Juan Lujan). Unfortunately this document has disappeared.

6. Lange and Riley, *Journals of Bandelier, 1883–1884*, p. 173.

7. J. Espinosa, *Spanish Folk-Tales*, p. 173.

8. Parsons, *Social Organization of the Tewa*, pp. 304–06.

Chapter 7: The Zuñi Plague of Witches

1. Frank H. Cushing, *My Adventures in Zuñi*, Introduction by Oakah L. Jones (Palmer Lake, Colorado, 1967), p. v.

2. Stevenson, *The Zuñi Indians*, p. 32.

3. Parsons, "Witchcraft Among the Pueblos," p. 204.

4. *Ibid.*, pp. 204–05.

5. Stevenson, *The Zuñi Indians*, p. 393.

6. Lange and Riley, *Journals of Bandelier, 1883–1884*, p. 29.

7. John Upton Terrell, *Estevanico the Black* (Los Angeles, 1968), pp. 136–37.

8. *SANM*, II, doc. no. 1673, "Official Daily Reports of the Governor's Office," June 21–August 29, 1803.

9. Hawley, "Mechanics of Pueblo Witchcraft," p. 153.

10. Parsons, "Witchcraft Among the Pueblos," p. 205n.

11. Ruth L. Bunzel, *Introduction to Zuñi Ceremonialism* (Washington, D.C., 1929), p. 479.

12. Cushing, *My Adventures in Zuñi*, pp. 44–45.

13. Stevenson, *The Zuñi Indians*, pp. 398–406.

14. George Wharton James, *New Mexico, The Land of the Delight Makers* (Boston, 1920), pp. 86–91; and Arthur Woodward, "Concerning Witches," *Masterkey*, 24 (1950):187–88.

15. Stevenson, *The Zuñi Indians*, p. 406.

16. James, *New Mexico*, pp. 91–92.

17. "Mechanics of Pueblo Witchcraft," p. 143.

18. Woodward, "Concerning Witches," pp. 183–87.

19. Parsons, "Witchcraft Among the Pueblos," pp. 204–09.

20. Account of J. F. Ealy, *Annual Report of Commissioner of Indian Affairs, 1880* (Washington, D.C., 1881), p. 135.

21. Stevenson, *The Zuñi Indians*, p. 394.

22. *Ibid.*, pp. 394–95.

Chapter 8: Montezuma, A Sacred Snake, and Pecos Pueblo

1. Twitchell, *Leading Facts*, I, pp. 402–03; and Rozier Paul Hughes, "The Legend of Montezuma," *Santa Fe Magazine*, 26 (1932):27–31.

2. Hammond and Rey, *Benavides' Revised Memorial of 1634*, pp. 40–41.

3. *Relaciones* (Albuquerque, 1966), p. 91.

4. Bancroft, *History of Arizona and New Mexico*, p. 181.

5. A. W. Whipple, *Report Upon the Indian Tribes* (Washington, D.C., 1855), p. 36.

6. John E. Sunder, ed., *Matt Field on the Santa Fe Trail* (Norman, Oklahoma, 1960), pp. 184–86.

7. *Commerce of the Prairies* (Norman, Oklahoma, 1954), p. 189.

8. Applegate, *Indian Stories*, p. 177.

9. Gregg, *Commerce of the Prairies*, p. 189.

10. John Galvin, ed., *Western America in 1846–1847* (San Francisco, 1966), p. 41.

11. Gregg, *Commerce of the Prairies*, p. 189–90.

12. Galvin, *Western America*, p. 41.

13. Alfred V. Kidder, *The Story of the Pueblo of Pecos* (Santa Fe, 1951), p. 9.

14. Helen H. Roberts, "The Reason for the Departure of the Pecos Indians for Jemez Pueblo," *American Anthropologist*, 34 (1932):359–60.

15. Jaramillo, *Shadows of the Past*, pp. 18–19.

16. Frank McNitt, *Navajo Expedition* (Norman, Oklahoma, 1964), p. 79.

Chapter 9: Navajo and Apache Witchcraft

1. Gladys A. Reichard, "The Navajo and Christianity," *American Anthropologist*, 51 (1949):67.

2. Ruth F. Kirk, "Designs for Magic," *New Mexico Magazine*, 18 (1940):15. See also Aileen O'Bryan, *The Diné: Origin Myths of the Navajo Indians* (Washington, D.C., 1956).

3. Gladys A. Reichard, *Navajo Religion*, 2nd ed. (New York, 1963), p. 16.

4. *Ibid.*, p. 105.

5. Sandy Hassell, *Know the Navajo* (Estes Park, Colorado, 1966), pp. 5, 38–39.

6. Dane and Mary Roberts Coolidge, *The Navajo Indians* (New York, 1930), p. 144; and Hassell, *Know the Navajo*, p. 36.

7. Kluckhohn, *Navajo Witchcraft*, p. 26.

8. Reichard, *Navajo Religion*, p. 40.

9. Kirk, "Designs for Magic," p. 38.

10. Kluckhohn, *Navajo Witchcraft*, p. 27.

11. Kirk, "Designs for Magic," p. 15.

12. Reichard, *Navajo Religion*, pp. 88–89.

13. Kluckhohn, *Navajo Witchcraft*, p. 26.

14. *Santa Fe Daily New Mexican*, May 23, 1895.

15. Lange and Riley, *Journals of Bandelier, 1883–1884*, p. 158.

16. Coolidge, *The Navajo Indians*, p. 155; and Kluckhohn, *Navajo Witchcraft*, pp. 46–47.

18. Erna Fergusson, *Dancing Gods* (Albuquerque, 1966), p. 199.

19. Kluckhohn, *Navajo Witchcraft*, pp. 156–57.

20. *Ibid.*, pp. 155–56.

21. Keith H. Basso, "Western Apache Witchcraft," in Deward E. Walker, Jr., ed., *Systems of North American Witchcraft and Sorcery* (Moscow, Idaho, 1970), pp. 17–18.

22. Morris E. Opler, *Apache Odyssey* (New York, 1969), pp. 71–74.

Chapter 10: Herbalism and Black Magic

1. Bourke, "Superstitions of the Rio Grande," p. 143.

2. L. S. M. Curtin, *Healing Herbs of the Upper Rio Grande* (Santa Fe, 1947), p. 45.

3. *Ibid.*, pp. 117–18.
4. Goldfrank, *Social Organization of Cochiti*, p. 95.
5. Lange, *Cochiti*, pp. 93–94.
6. Reichard, *Navajo Religion*, p. 109.
7. Bourke, "Superstitions on the Rio Grande," p. 143.
8. Florence H. Ellis, "Pueblo Witchcraft and Medicine," in Walker, *Systems of North American Witchcraft and Sorcery*, p. 52.
9. Leslie A. White, *The Pueblo of Zia, New Mexico* (Washington, D.C., 1962), p. 289.
10. Goldfrank, *Social Organization of Cochiti*, p. 95.
11. Hawley, "Mechanics of Pueblo Witchcraft," pp. 146–47.
12. Ellis, "Pueblo Witchcraft and Medicine," pp. 53–54.
13. Lange and Riley, *Journals of Bandelier, 1883–1884*, p. 158.
14. Jacques Soustelle, *La Vida Cotidiana de los Aztecas* (Mexico, 1956), p. 194.
15. Bunzel, *Zuñi Ceremonialism*, p. 533.
16. Quoted in Madsen, *Guide to Mexican Witchcraft*, p. 94.
17. Adrian García Cortes, *Los Huicholes* (Mexico, 1950), pp. 6–7.
18. Bennett and Zingg, *The Tarahumara*, pp. 294–95.
19. Two standard works on the subject are Weston La Barre, *The Peyote Cult* (New Haven, 1933); and J. S. Slotkin, *The Peyote Religion* (Glencoe, Illinois, 1956). See also the recent study by Alice Marriott and Carol K. Rachlin, *Peyote* (New York, 1971).
20. These cases from the Inquisition papers in the Archivo General de la Nación, Mexico City, appear in translation in Scholes, "First Decade of the Inquisition," p. 232.
21. Ellis, "Pueblo Witchcraft and Medicine," p. 51.
22. Curtin, *Healing Herbs*, pp. 185–86.
23. *Ibid.*, p. 186.
24. Ruth Laughlin Barker, *Caballeros* (New York, 1936), p. 280.
25. Kluckhohn, *Navajo Witchcraft*, p. 40.
26. *Ibid.*, p. 175; and W. W. Hill, "Navajo Use of Jimson Weed," *New Mexico Anthropologist*, 3 (1938):19–21.
27. Barker, "New Mexico Witch Tales," pp. 64–65.
28. Wilson M. Hudson, ed., *The Healer of Los Olmos* (Dallas, 1951), pp. 9–26.
29. See especially Madsen, *Mexican-Americans*, pp. 80–86; Rubel, *Across the Tracks*, pp. 155–92; and Ari Kiev, *Curanderismo, Mexican-American Folk Psychiatry* (New York, 1968).
30. Hurtado, *Medicina Popular de Navarra*, pp. 12–13.
31. Max Evans, "Witches' Brew," *True West*, March-April, 1957, p. 17.
32. Jaramillo, *Shadows of the Past*, pp. 100–01.
33. J. Espinosa, *Spanish Folk-Tales*, p. 172.

Chapter 11: The Lingering Legacy of Witchcraft

1. *Albuquerque Journal*, June 8, 1955.
2. *Our Southwest* (New York, 1946), p. 254.
3. Hurt, "Witchcraft in New Mexico," p. 74.
4. *Santa Fe New Mexican*, July 25, 1966.
5. *Ibid.*, July 29, 1966.
6. Madsen, *Mexican-Americans*, p. 83.
7. Hurt, "Witchcraft in New Mexico," p. 81.
8. Evans, "Witches' Brew," p. 17.
9. Rubel, *Across the Tracks*, p. 161.
10. Fergusson, *Our Southwest*, p. 254.
11. "Felicia the Bruja," *WPA Papers*.
12. Hurt, "Witchcraft in New Mexico," p. 74.
13. Bourke, "Superstitions on the Rio Grande," p. 142.
14. Ellis, "Pueblo Witchcraft and Medicine," p. 69.
15. Madsen, *Mexican-Americans*, p. 80.
16. A. Espinosa, "New Mexican Spanish Folklore," p. 398.
17. *Navajo Witchcraft*, pp. 14, 18.
18. A. Espinosa, "New Mexican Spanish Folklore," pp. 404–05.
19. Mackay, *Extraordinary Popular Delusions*, p. 468.
20. Jaramillo, *Shadows of the Past*, p. 105.
21. A. Espinosa, "New Mexican Spanish Folklore," p. 403.
22. Elsa and Omar Barker, "La Llorona," *True West*, September-October, 1972, p. 39.
23. Hudson, *Healer of Los Olmos*, p. 73.
24. Betty Leddy, "La Llorona in Southern Arizona," *Western Folklore*, 7 (1948):272–77.
25. Bourke, "Superstitions of the Rio Grande," p. 142; and A. Espinosa, "New Mexican Spanish Folklore," pp. 410–11.

Bibliography

Adams, Eleanor B. and Fray Angélico Chávez, eds. *The Missions of New Mexico, 1776*. Albuquerque, 1956.

Applegate, Frank. *Indian Stories from the Pueblos*. Philadelphia, 1929.

Bancroft, Hubert Howe. *History of Arizona and New Mexico*. San Francisco, 1889.

Barker, Elsa and Omar. "La Llorona," *True West*, September-October, 1972, p. 39.

Barker, Ruth Laughlin, *Caballeros*. New York, 1936.

Barker, Ruth Laughlin. "New Mexico Witch Tales," in J. Frank Dobie, ed. *Tone the Bell Easy*. Austin, 1932, pp. 62–70.

Basso, Keith H. "Western Apache Witchcraft," in Deward E. Walker, Jr. ed. *Systems of North American Witchcraft and Sorcery*. Moscow, Idaho, 1970, pp. 11–36.

Bennett, Wendell C. and Robert M. Zingg. *The Tarahumara, An Indian Tribe of Northern Mexico*. Chicago, 1935.

Bourke, John G. "Superstitions of the Rio Grande," *Journal of American Folklore*, 7 (1894):122–46.

Bunzel, Ruth L. *Introduction to Zuñi Ceremonialism*. Washington, D.C., 1929.

Chávez, Fray Angélico. *Archives of the Archdiocese of Santa Fe*. Washington, D.C., 1957.

Chávez, Fray Angélico. *Origins of New Mexico Families*. Santa Fe, 1954.

Chávez, Fray Angélico. "Pohe-yemo's Representative and the Pueblo Revolt of 1680," *New Mexico Historical Review*, 42 (1967):85–126.

Chávez, Tibo J. "Early Witchcraft in New Mexico," *El Palacio*, 77 (1970):7–9.

Coolidge, Dane and Mary Roberts. *The Navajo Indians*. New York, 1930.

Curtin, L. S. M. *Healing Herbs of the Upper Rio Grande*. Santa Fe, 1947.

Curtin, L. S. M. "Spanish and Indian Witchcraft in New Mexico," *Masterkey*, 40 (1971):89–101.

Cushing, Frank H. *My Adventures in Zuñi*. Palmer Lake, Colorado, 1967.

Davis, W. W. H. *El Gringo*. Santa Fe, 1938.

DeHuff, Elizabeth Willis. "Where Witches Abound," *Southwest Review*, 11 (1926):253–63.

Dumarest, Noel. *Notes on Cochití, New Mexico*. Menasha, Wisconsin, 1919.

Espinosa, Aurelio. "New Mexican Spanish Folklore," *Journal of American Folklore*, 23 (1910): 395-418.

Espinosa, José Manuel. *Spanish Folk-Tales From New Mexico*. New York, 1937.

Evans, Max. "Witches' Brew," *True West*, March-April, 1957, p. 17.

Fergusson, Erna. *Dancing Gods*. Albuquerque, 1966.

Fox, J. Robin. "Witchcraft and Clanship in Cochití Therapy," in John Middleton, ed. *Magic, Witchcraft, and Curing*. New York, 1967, pp. 255–84.

Galvin, John, ed. *Western America in 1846–1847*. San Francisco, 1966.

García Cortes, Adrian. *Los Huicholes*. Mexico, 1950.

Gifford, Edward S., Jr. *The Evil Eye, Studies in the Folklore of Vision*. New York, 1958.

Goldfrank, Esther S. *The Social and Ceremonial Organization of Cochití*. Menasha, Wisconsin, 1927.

Gregg, Josiah. *Commerce of the Prairies*. Norman, Oklahoma, 1954.

Hammond, George P. and Agapito Rey, eds. *Fray Alonso de Benavides' Revised Memorial of 1634*. Albuquerque, 1945.

Hansen, Chadwick. *Witchcraft at Salem*. New York, 1969.

Hassell, Sandy. *Know the Navajo*. Estes Park, Colorado, 1966.

Hawley, Florence. "The Mechanics of Perpetuation in Pueblo Witchcraft," in Erik K. Reed and Dale S. King, eds. *For the Dean*. Santa Fe, 1950, pp. 143–58.

Hodge, Frederick Webb, ed. *Handbook of American Indians North of Mexico*. 2 vols. New York, 1971.

Hodge, Frederick Webb and Charles Fletcher Lummis, eds. *The Memorial of Fray Alonso de Benavides, 1630*. Chicago, 1916.

Hudson, Wilson M., ed. *The Healer of Los Olmos*. Dallas, 1951.

Hurt, Wesley R., Jr. "Witchcraft in New Mexico," *El Palacio*, 47 (1940): 73–83.

Hurtado de Saracho, Arántzazu. *Medicina Popular de Navarra*. Pamplona, 1968.

James, George Wharton. *New Mexico, Land of the Delight Makers*. Boston, 1920.

Jaramillo, Cleofas M. *Shadows of the Past*. Santa Fe, 1972.

Kamen, Henry. *The Spanish Inquisition*. New York, 1965.

Kidder, Alfred V. *The Story of the Pueblo of Pecos*. Santa Fe, 1951.

Kiev, Ari. *Curanderismo, Mexican-American Folk Psychiatry*. New York, 1968.

Kirk, Ruth L. "Designs for Magic," *New Mexico Magazine*, 18 (1940): 14.

Kluckhohn, Clyde. *Navajo Witchcraft*. Boston, 1967.

Lange, Charles H. *Cochití, A New Mexico Pueblo, Past and Present*. Austin, 1959.

Lange, Charles H. and Carroll L. Riley, eds. *The Southwestern Journals of Adolph F. Bandelier, 1883–1884*. Albuquerque, 1970.

Leddy, Betty. "La Llorona in Southern Arizona," *Western Folklore*, 12 (1948): 272–77.

Lummis, Charles F. *Mesa, Cañon, and Pueblo*. New York, 1925.

Lummis, Charles F. *A New Mexico David*. New York, 1916.

Lummis, Charles F. *Some Strange Corners of Our Country*. New York, 1892.

Lummis, Charles F. *A Tramp Across the Continent*. New York, 1920.

[Lummis, Charles F.] "Witchcraft in New Mexico," *Journal of American Folklore*, 1 (1888): 75–76.

Mackay, Charles. *Extraordinary Popular Delusions and the Madness of Crowds*. New York, 1932.

Madsen, William. *The Mexican-Americans of South Texas*. New York, 1964.

Madsen, William and Claudia. *A Guide to Mexican Witchcraft*. Mexico, 1969.

Murray, Margaret. *The God of the Witches*. London, 1933.

Ortiz, Alfonso. "Ritual Drama and the Pueblo World View," in Alfonso Ortiz, ed. *New Perspectives on the Pueblos*. Albuquerque, 1972, pp. 135–61.

Parsons, Elsie C. *Isleta*. Washington, D.C., 1932.

Parsons, Elsie C. *Notes on Zuñi*. Menasha, Wisconsin, 1917.

Parsons, Elsie C. *The Pueblo of Jémez*. New Haven, 1925.

Parsons, Elsie C. *Pueblo Religion*. 2 vols. Chicago, 1939.

Parsons, Elsie C. *The Social Organization of the Tewa of New Mexico*. Menasha, Wisconsin, 1929.

Parsons, Elsie C. "Witchcraft Among the Pueblos: Indian or Spanish?" in Max Marwick, ed. *Witchcraft and Sorcery*. Baltimore, 1970.

Rael, Juan B. *Cuentos Españoles de Colorado y de Nuevo Méjico*. 2 vols. Stanford, n.d.

Reichard, Gladys A. *Navajo Religion*. 2nd ed. New York, 1963.

Reichard, Gladys A. "The Navajo and Christianity," *American Anthropologist*, 51 (1949): 66–71.

Roberts, Helen H. "The Reason for the Departure of the Pecos Indians for Jémez Pueblo," *American Anthropologist*, 34 (1932): 359–60.

Roth, Cecil. *The Spanish Inquisition*. New York, 1964.

Rubel, Arthur J. *Across the Tracks, Mexican-Americans in a Texas City*. Austin, 1966.

SANM [Spanish Archives of New Mexico], State Records Center, Santa Fe.

Scholes, France V. "The First Decade of the Inquisition in New Mexico," *New Mexico Historical Review*, 10 (1935): 195–241.

Seligmann, Kurt. *Magic, Supernaturalism, and Religion*. New York, 1968.

Seth, Ronald. *Witches and Their Craft*. New York, 1968.

Soustelle, Jacques. *La Vida Cotidiana de los Aztecas*. Mexico, 1956.

Stevenson, Matilda Coxe. *The Zuñi Indians*. Washington, D.C., 1905.

Sunder, John E., ed. *Matt Field on the Santa Fe Trail*. Norman, Oklahoma, 1960.

Tedlock, Dennis, "Pueblo Literature: Style and Verisimilitude." in Ortiz, *New Perspectives on the Pueblos*, pp. 219–42.

Terrell, John Upton. *Estevanico The Black*. Los Angeles, 1968.

Tuberville, A. S. *La Inquisición Española*. Mexico, 1948.

Twitchell, Ralph Emerson. *The Leading Facts of New Mexican History*. 2 vols. Albuquerque, 1963.

Walker, Deward E., Jr., ed. *Systems of North American Witchcraft and Sorcery*. Moscow, Idaho, 1970.

Whipple, A. W. *Report Upon the Indian Tribes*. Washington, D.C., 1855.

White, Leslie A. *The Acoma Indians*. Washington, D.C., 1932.

White, Leslie A. *The Pueblo of Zia, New Mexico*. Washington, D.C., 1962.

WPA [Works Progress Administration]. Unpublished manuscripts in files of Museum of New Mexico, Santa Fe.

Woodward, Arthur. "Concerning Witches," *Masterkey*, 24 (1950): 187–88.

Zárate Salmerón, Fray Gerónimo de. *Relaciones*. Albuquerque, 1966.